FLOYD CLYMER'S MOTORCYCLIST'S LIBRARY

The Book of the
ARIEL

A PRACTICAL GUIDE FOR OWNERS
OF SINGLE-CYLINDER S.V., O.H.V.
FOUR-STROKE TOURING MODELS
(1939 TO 1960)

BY

W. C. HAYCRAFT
F.R.S.A.

ANNOUNCEMENT

By special arrangement with the original publishers of this book, Sir Isaac Pitman & Son, Ltd., of London, England, we have secured the exclusive publishing rights for this book, as well as all others in THE MOTORCYCLIST'S LIBRARY.

Included in THE MOTORCYCLIST'S LIBRARY are complete instruction manuals covering the care and operation of respective motorcycles and engines; valuable data on speed tuning, and thrilling accounts of motorcycle race events. See listing of available titles elsewhere in this edition.

We consider it a privilege to be able to offer so many fine titles to our customers.

FLOYD CLYMER
Publisher of Books Pertaining to Automobiles and Motorcycles
2125 W. PICO ST.   LOS ANGELES 6, CALIF.

INTRODUCTION

Welcome to the world of digital publishing ~ the book you now hold in your hand, while unchanged from the original edition, was printed using the latest state of the art digital technology. The advent of print-on-demand has forever changed the publishing process, never has information been so accessible and it is our hope that this book serves your informational needs for years to come. If this is your first exposure to digital publishing, we hope that you are pleased with the results. Many more titles of interest to the classic automobile and motorcycle enthusiast, collector and restorer are available via our website at www.VelocePress.com. We hope that you find this title as interesting as we do.

NOTE FROM THE PUBLISHER

The information presented is true and complete to the best of our knowledge. All recommendations are made without any guarantees on the part of the author or the publisher, who also disclaim all liability incurred with the use of this information.

TRADEMARKS

We recognize that some words, model names and designations, for example, mentioned herein are the property of the trademark holder. We use them for identification purposes only. This is not an official publication.

INFORMATION ON THE USE OF THIS PUBLICATION

This manual is an invaluable resource for the classic motorcycle enthusiast and a "must have" for owners interested in performing their own maintenance. However, in today's information age we are constantly subject to changes in common practice, new technology, availability of improved materials and increased awareness of chemical toxicity. As such, it is advised that the user consult with an experienced professional prior to undertaking any procedure described herein. While every care has been taken to ensure correctness of information, it is obviously not possible to guarantee complete freedom from errors or omissions or to accept liability arising from such errors or omissions. Therefore, any individual that uses the information contained within, or elects to perform or participate in do-it-yourself repairs or modifications acknowledges that there is a risk factor involved and that the publisher or its associates cannot be held responsible for personal injury or property damage resulting from the use of the information or the outcome of such procedures.

WARNING!

One final word of advice, this publication is intended to be used as a reference guide, and when in doubt the reader should consult with a qualified technician.

PREFACE

THE purpose of this handbook is to provide comprehensive instructions on the handling and general maintenance of *all* 1939–60 single-cylinder side-valve and overhead-valve four-stroke Ariel motor-cycles. The instructions are written in simple language and are for the benefit of experienced and inexperienced motor-cyclists. These instructions should help you to obtain the maximum pleasure, mileage, m.p.g., and m.p.£. from your Ariel mount, and also reduce its annual depreciation.

The handbook does *not* deal with O.H.V. four-cylinder models and vertical twins, nor with two-stroke, Trials and Scrambles models. The touring models fully covered are—

1. The 1939–49 250 c.c. O.H.V. Models OG, OH.
2. The 1939–49 500 c.c. S.V. Model VA.
3. The 1939–50 500 c.c. O.H.V. Model VG.
4. The 1939–50 350 c.c. O.H.V. Model NG.
5. The 1939–60 350 c.c. O.H.V. Model NH ("Red Hunter").
6. The 1939–60 500 c.c. O.H.V. Model VH ("Red Hunter").
7. The 1952–3 500 c.c. O.H.V. Model VHA ("Red Hunter").
8. The 1939–58 600 c.c. S.V. Model VB.
9. The 1954–60 200 c.c. O.H.V. Model LH ("Colt").

The author regrets to say that subsequent to 1960 the production of *all* Ariel single-cylinder four-stroke models has ceased. During the period 1958–64 the popular 247 c.c. twin-cylinder two-stroke models (the Leader and Arrow) were marketed. These machines, whose production has also now ceased, are dealt with in another Pitman handbook.

Many of the instructions in the maintenance sections of this handbook are dated to ensure quick reference in the lock-up shed or garage. Where the instructions are not dated, they apply to *all* 1939–60 O.H.V. singles. If you have never before handled an Ariel, turn direct to Chapter I which deals with preliminaries, starting-up, and riding.

In conclusion I thank Ariel Motors, Ltd. (now amalgamated with B.S.A. Motor Cycles, Ltd.) of Small Heath, Birmingham, 11, for their helpful assistance in regard to technical data, and for kindly permitting various Ariel illustrations to be reproduced. The same also applies to the makers of various excellent accessories.

W.C.H.

CONTENTS

CHAP.		PAGE
I.	HANDLING AN ARIEL	1
II.	CORRECT CARBURATION	19
III.	THE LIGHTING EQUIPMENT	30
IV.	ARIEL LUBRICATION	54
V.	GENERAL MAINTENANCE	77
	Index	143

CHAPTER I

HANDLING AN ARIEL

BECAUSE this handbook is concerned mainly with maintenance, and space at the author's disposal is limited, it is only possible to refer briefly to actual riding and to cover the lay-out and handling of Ariel controls. It is not practicable to include detailed information on the technique of riding, legal matters, etc. Do not omit to read a copy of *The Highway Code*. Wear a crash helmet.

Important Preliminaries Outlined. Before you can legally get on the road astride a brand new or good second-hand Ariel, you must attend to the following essential preliminaries—

1. Insure against all *third-party* risks and obtain the vital "certificate of insurance." With a new machine you cannot obtain this until the machine has been registered and a registration number is allocated to it. Pending this, obtain an insurance "cover note." If a machine is purchased on a hire-purchase agreement, you will be obliged to take out a full comprehensive insurance policy. This type of policy is always advised in the case of a valuable machine.

2. Obtain the registration book and the registration licence (Form R.F.1/A for renewal, and Form R.F. 1/2* for original registration or change of ownership). All S.V. and O.H.V. singles except the 200 c.c. O.H.V. Ariel "Colt" are taxed at the annual rate of £8 (no extra for a sidecar). The 200 c.c. Ariel "Colt" (Model LH) has an annual tax of £4.

3. If you are a "learner," take out a "provisional" (six months) licence; otherwise obtain a "full" three-year driving licence. Note that a "provisional" licence holder must not ride a solo machine exceeding 250 c.c. capacity. The correct Form in both cases is D.L.1. Immediately you get the appropriate licence, *sign it*. Note that you are not legally entitled to a three-year licence until you are 16 (for Group G) and have complied with one of these conditions—
   (*a*) You have held a licence (other than a provisional or Visitor's licence)

---

* Note that on Form R.F.1/2 you must state the engine and frame numbers (with prefix letters), which are located on the near-side of the crankcase just below the cylinder-barrel flange, and on the near-side of the steering-head lug, respectively.

authorizing the driving of vehicles of the class or description applied for within a period of ten years ending on the date of coming into force of the licence applied for.

(b) You have passed the prescribed driving test (which includes a test passed while serving in H.M. Forces) during the said period of ten years.

FIG. 1. TYPICAL OF THE 1959 ARIEL O.H.V. SINGLES—THE POPULAR 350 C.C. MODEL NH "RED HUNTER" WHICH COMBINES SPARKLING PERFORMANCE WITH GENUINE RELIABILITY AND ECONOMY

This modern "three-fifty," like the other two Ariel singles, remains unchanged since 1957. Its maximum speed is 75–80 m.p.h. and fuel consumption averages 85–90 m.p.g. Its fully-laden weight is most reasonable—365 lb. Specification details of this mount and the 500-c.c. Model VH (both of which have an aluminium-alloy cylinder head) are really excellent, and modernization has not been overdone. The other Ariel single comprises the sturdy 200 c.c. O.H.V. Model LH, weighing only 270 lb, and with a top speed of 55–60 m.p.h.

4. Fit a reliable speedometer, if one is not already fitted, to show within ± 10 per cent accuracy when 30 m.p.h. is being exceeded. On 1939–50 O.H.V. and S.V. singles the speedometer is normally mounted on the off-side of the large instrument panel fitted to the top of the petrol tank; on all later models the speedometer is mounted above the telescopic-type front forks.

5. If you are not eligible for an annual or a three-year driving licence,

to the front and rear of the motor-cycle, and see that they are properly secured. Later apply for a driving test (Form D.L.26).

6. Where a pillion passenger is carried, see that he or she sits *astride* a proper pillion seat securely *fixed* to the machine. Ariel "springers" have, of course, dualseats fitted. Note that in the event of your holding only a "provisional" licence, the pillion rider must possess a "full" driving licence (not a "provisional" one) covering Group G vehicles.

7. Where your mount was first registered subsequent to 1st July, 1953, see that the engine has an "ignition-supression" type sparking plug or else a terminal cover of the same type, designed to prevent interference with radio and television sets.

8. See that a red reflector (of $1\frac{1}{2}$ in. minimum diameter) is fitted to the rear of a solo motor-cycle in addition to (or combined with) the tail lamp or stop-tail lamp. Where a sidecar is attached, this must carry an additional red reflector at the rear at the same height as the reflector on the motor-cycle, and an extra tail lamp must also be provided.

Note that the official forms mentioned in paragraphs 2, 3, and 5 are obtainable from any money-order post office.

The Ariel Riding Position. On a new machine the standard position is generally found to be suitable for a man of average build, but to suit those not of average physique, it is possible on most machines to make a combined adjustment of the handlebars, footrests, and some of the handlebar controls. It is well worth while ensuring that the riding position *is* the best obtainable. The hands should come down readily on the handlebars and the arms be practically straight; the angle between each thigh and foot should be slightly less than a right-angle.

Footrest Adjustment. Adjust each footrest to suit your own physique and comfort, giving nice easy action of the foot gear-change lever and the rear-brake pedal. To remove a footrest for adjustment, take off its securing nut and tap the footrest along the splined or serrated tube. After replacing the footrest, tighten the securing nut very firmly.

LAY-OUT AND USE OF CONTROLS

The Control Lay-out. It is assumed that you are familiar with general engine principles and comprehend the functions of the various engine and motor-cycle controls, which are more or less the same on all four-stroke singles. Should you be a novice, it is a sound plan to sit on the saddle, manipulate the controls, and carefully consider the effect of doing this with the engine running. Before starting up the engine a proper understanding of the controls is essential. The location of the handlebar controls is clearly shown in the accompanying illustrations, and the appropriate lay-out should be thoroughly memorized.

Notes on the Use of Ariel Controls. All Ariel riders (particularly novices) should carefully memorize and observe the following important points—

1. The handlebar controls (including the throttle twist-grip) are all operated by *inward movement*.

FIG. 2. A GOOD ARIEL EXTRA—A FINE ADJUSTABLE WINDSCREEN

Above is shown a specially designed "Golden Peacock" windscreen supplied and strongly recommended by Ariel dealers for all Ariel motor-cycles. Its price is reasonable and it affords excellent protection against the elements. With this windscreen fitted, no goggles are necessary and stability, riding tactics, and noise are not appreciably affected. Another worth-while extra is a substantial design of safety bars. Both extras are readily fitted or removed and contribute to road safety

2. The throttle twist-grip (which controls engine speed) has a full movement of about *one-quarter of a complete turn*. When the throttle-stop on the carburettor is adjusted to give a good tick-over at medium speed with the throttle twist-grip completely closed, the throttle slide does not itself shut completely and will not stop the engine.

On starting up an Ariel engine *from cold* it is essential always to open the throttle twist-grip *very slightly* (about one-eighth of its total movement), otherwise quick starting is most unlikely to occur. The most satisfactory twist-grip position can soon be judged by experiment.

3. Always keep the air lever (omitted on the 1954–9 200 c.c. Ariel O.H.V. "Colts") *fully open* except when starting up the engine, and perhaps immediately after starting up; until an engine attains its normal running temperature (usually within about half a minute) it is often desirable to keep the air lever *half to three-quarters open*. When starting up a *cold engine* close the air lever *completely* (push fully forward), and when starting up a *warm engine* open the air lever *about one-third to one-half of its total movement*.

4. The ignition lever (omitted on 1954–60 200 c.c. O.H.V. "Colts" with automatic-ignition advance) turns the contact-breaker base relative to the actuating cam, and thereby advances or retards the ignition according to the direction of movement of the base. The ignition should always be kept *fully advanced while riding*, but if some "pinking" occurs while hill climbing, it is permissible to retard the ignition slightly and momentarily; remember that retarding the ignition (forward movement, 1956–9) inevitably reduces the power output of the engine. When *starting up* the engine, always retard the ignition lever so that it is approximately *one-third advanced*; this facilitates starting and avoids the risk of an unpleasant kick-back when operating the kick-starter.

5. An ignition switch is provided only on the 1954–60 200 c.c. O.H.V. "Colts" which have coil ignition. On 1954–5 "Colts" the switch comprises a detachable key mounted in the centre of the plastic lighting switch (*see* page 9) which is built into the upper side of the Wipac headlamp shell. Note that the ignition key can only be removed when the ignition is switched off.

On the 1956–60 "Colts" a separate plastic lighting switch (*see* page 9) is built into the headlamp shell close to, and to the right of the plastic ignition switch. The metal ignition key (1954–5 models) or plastic ignition switch (1956–60 models) has the following three consecutive positions—

"OFF." Ignition switched off; the ignition can be locked in this position, and the key removed.

"IGN." Ignition switched on.

"EMG." For starting up when in trouble with a flat battery or faulty rectifier; in this position a small charge is given to the Varley or Exide battery, and after a few minutes' running it is generally possible to move the ignition key or plastic switch to the normal "IGN" position. Observe that it is most unwise to ride for a lengthy period (*see* page 53) with the ignition key or plastic switch in the "EMG" (emergency) position.

6. Do not use the exhaust-valve lifter (omitted on 1954–60 200 c.c. O.H.V. "Colts") except for the purpose of stopping and starting the engine. It is permissible, however, when descending a long gradient to cool off a hot engine by raising the exhaust-valve lifter with the throttle twist-grip fully closed and the air lever wide open. This unorthodox procedure is, of

course, normally unnecessary and makes it impossible to employ engine compression for braking.

7. The clutch lever (which connects and disconnects the transmission from the engine to the rear wheel) must always be kept fully out, or squeezed fully inwards and then released (progressively) during each gear change, including changing into "neutral."

8. The foot gear-change pedal on the off-side of the Burman gearbox provides four gear ratios, and "neutral" which lies between first and second gears. It is necessary during each gear change to make a *full movement* of the gear-change pedal. The pedal always returns to the same position (nearly horizontal) after each gear change, ready for the next change to be made. To obtain *neutral* from first gear only *a very slight downward movement* of the gear-change pedal is necessary, but for all actual up gear changes a full downward movement of the pedal must be made with the toe. When changing down a similar upward movement must be made with the toe.

Filling Petrol Tank. It is highly desirable always to run on a good premium-grade petrol (e.g. B.P. Super), and the capacity of the petrol tank varies from about $2\frac{1}{2}$ gal. to $4\frac{1}{2}$ gal., according to the type of model and its date of manufacture. Petrol consumption, for similar reasons, varies from 70–75 m.p.g. (Model VB) to 100–110 m.p.g. (Model LH). 1939–50 models have an instrument panel on the tank and it houses the filler cap, oil-pressure gauge, etc.

All 1956–60 Ariel petrol tanks have a plain-top filler cap which can quickly be removed by turning it *anti-clockwise* until the catch is felt, pushing the cap down, and then turning it anti-clockwise as far as possible and lifting the cap off. To tighten the cap, push it down and then turn *clockwise* to the maximum extent. On 1939–55 Ariel tanks, however, the filler cap has a centre screw. To remove the filler cap, slacken the centre screw, turn the cap one-quarter of a turn *anti-clockwise*, and lift up. To replace the filler cap, drop it into position, turn the cap *clockwise* as far as possible, and finally tighten the centre screw.

Oil Replenishment. On no account ever economize in regard to engine oil. Only the correct grade of suitable engine oil (*see* page 58) will keep the engine cool and running at maximum efficiency, with the least amount of wear. On a new machine check that the level of oil in the oil tank is correct (*see* page 59), and afterwards regularly verify the level and change the oil periodically as described on page 64. The oil tank capacity varies from 4 pt. (Model LH) to 6 pt. (most other models), and oil consumption on a solo model should, given reasonable luck, average 2,000–2,500 m.p.g.

On a new Ariel, and subsequently at regular intervals, check that the Burman four-speed gearbox and the oil-bath primary-chain case are replenished with the correct amount and grade of engine oil (*see* page 69).

HANDLING AN ARIEL

Before riding see also that all other lubrication points (*see* lubrication chart on page 70) are properly attended to, and that the tyres are inflated to the correct pressures (*see* page 137). When riding a new motor-cycle away from an Ariel dealer the foregoing points are, of course, attended to as a normal routine; but such is not always the case where a new machine is delivered by rail or road transport. Here it is a good plan (if the new machine is a 200 c.c. "Colt") to commence getting ready for starting up by withdrawing the sparking plug and pouring a teaspoonful of the correct grade of engine oil (*see* page 58) into the cylinder bore. Replace the sparking plug, wait for several minutes, and then turn the engine over at a moderate speed with the kick-starter. This will provide a good film of protective oil between the cylinder-barrel surface and the piston rings.

Setting Controls for Starting (1939–60 Models OG, OH, VA, VG, NG, NH, VH, VHA, VB). Push your Ariel off its rear or spring-up centre stand, or alternatively keep the machine jacked up on its stand. If the machine is moved off its stand it is advisable to stand astride the machine, as this helps to balance it. Now turn on the petrol.

On a "Magdyno" model with a reserve petrol supply and a two-level type petrol tap, check that the main supply is turned on, unless this supply is exhausted; in this case turn the tap to the reserve position and replenish the petrol tank at the first opportunity. The two-level tap unit has *two knobs*. To turn on the main supply, pull out the knob "Pull on." To turn on the reserve petrol supply, pull out the knob "Pull reserve." For starting and while riding, always leave the knob "Pull on" fully pulled out. To shut off the petrol supply, *push in both knobs*.

Having turned on the main petrol supply, set the controls for starting up in the following manner—

1. Check that the foot gear-change mechanism is in "neutral" (*see* Figs. 7 and 8). It is advisable to verify that the rear wheel is quite free to rotate, or else observe the position of the indicator on the gearbox.

2. Retard the ignition lever so that it is about *two-thirds* retarded. On all except recent S.V. and O.H.V. models (*see* Fig. 4) *pull* the ignition lever *inwards* from the fully-advanced position; on all the recent models (*see* Fig. 3) *push* the ignition lever *outwards* to retard the ignition.

3. Open the throttle very slightly by turning the twist-grip *anti-clockwise* about *one-eighth* of its total movement.

4. Close the air lever completely unless the engine is *warm* (in which case open it about *one-third to one-half* of its total movement).

5. If the engine is quite *cold*, momentarily depress the "tickler" on the float chamber of the Amal carburettor, but avoid flooding the carburettor so that petrol begins to drip from it in an excessive manner. In the event of the engine being warm, do not touch the "tickler," or an over-rich mixture will result, causing difficulty in starting up.

You are now ready to start up, but if about to do this in a lock-up shed

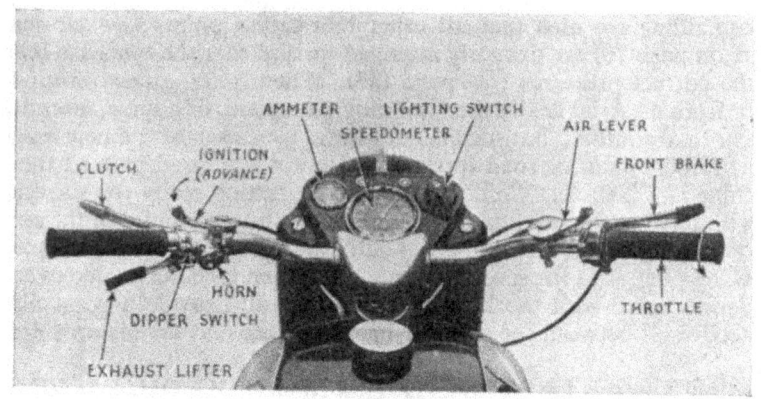

FIG. 3. LAY-OUT OF HANDLEBAR CONTROLS ON THE 1956-60 O.H.V. MODELS NH, VH, AND THE 1956-8 S.V. MODEL V.B.

The ammeter, lighting switch, and speedometer are mounted on a neat panel over the front forks. On these models the ignition lever is advanced by inward movement as indicated

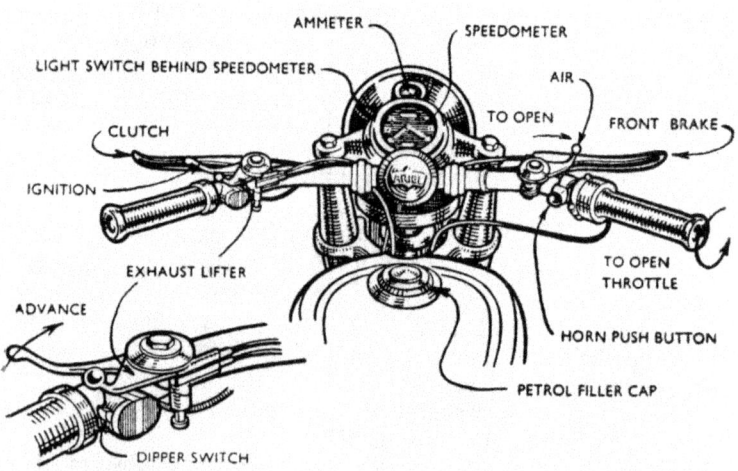

FIG. 4. LAY-OUT OF HANDLEBAR CONTROLS ON THE 1951-5 O.H.V. MODELS NH, VH, VAH, AND THE 1951-5 S.V. MODEL VB

Note that on these models the ignition lever is advanced by outward movement as indicated in the lower left-hand sketch

or small garage, first be sure that the door is *not* closed, invisible carbon monoxide fumes being extremely dangerous, and even lethal in a confined space.

Setting Controls for Starting (1954–60 O.H.V. MODEL LH). Before attempting to start up the engine of a "Colt," check that the petrol tank is

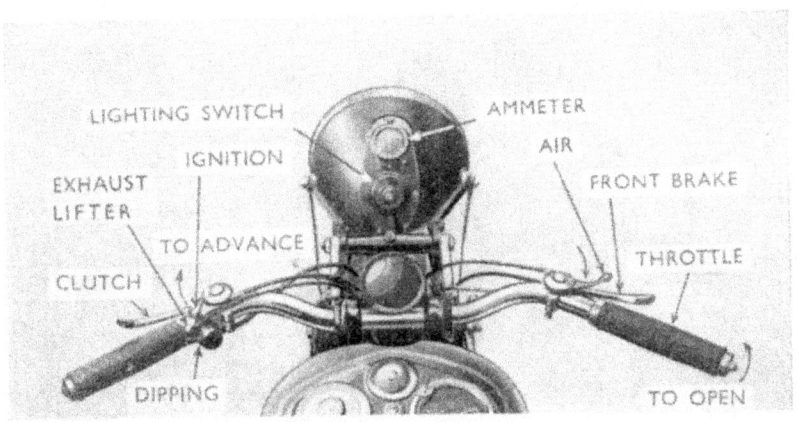

FIG. 5. LAY-OUT OF HANDLEBAR CONTROLS ON THE 1939–50 O.H.V. MODELS OG, OH, VG, NG, NH, VH, AND THE 1939–50 S.V. MODEL VB

On these models the ammeter and lighting switch are on a panel fitted to the head-lamp; the petrol tank filler-cap, speedometer, clock, oil-pressure gauge, and speedometer are mounted on an instrument panel screwed to the top of the petrol tank. As indicated, the ignition lever is advanced by outward movement

filled and oil replenishment correctly attended to (*see* page 6). Push your "Colt" off its spring-up centre stand, or move it off the stand and stand astride the machine. Next pull "ON" fully the petrol tap plunger.

If the level of the main petrol-supply happens to be low, turn the plunger *clockwise* (with the plunger fully out) to obtain the reserve supply, and then give it a further slight pull to lock the plunger in position.

Having turned on the main petrol-supply, adjust the various controls on the "Colt" as follows—

1. Make quite sure that the foot gear-change pedal has been moved so that "neutral" is engaged (*see* paragraph 1 on page 7).

2. Slightly open the twist-grip throttle control by turning it *anti-clockwise* about *one-eighth* of its total movement.

3. If the engine is quite *cold*, depress momentarily and gently the "tickler" on the carburettor float-chamber. Avoid actual flooding.

4. Switch on the ignition by turning the detachable ignition key (1954–5 models) or the separate plastic ignition switch (1956–60 models) so that the key or switch is in the "IGN" position; if the battery is flat for some

reason, turn the ignition switch to the "EMG" position (*see* paragraph 5 on page 5).

Kick-starting (All 1939–60 Singles Except 1954–60 200 c.c. "Colts"). Having correctly adjusted the handlebar controls and engaged "neutral," push down the kick-starter until the strong resistance of engine compression is felt. Then allow the kick-starter to return to the top of its travel.

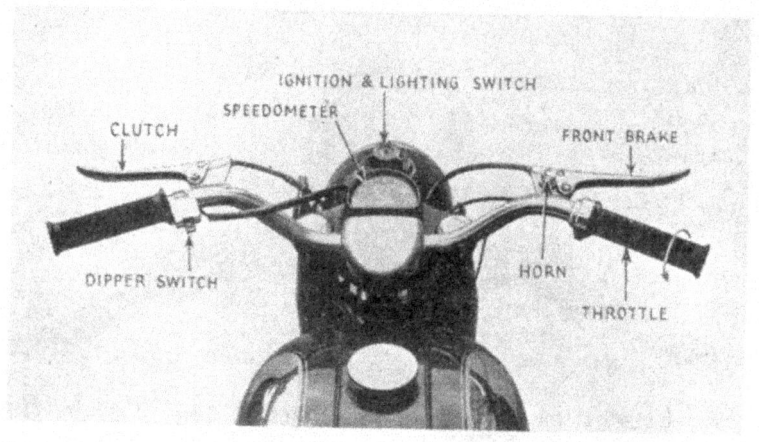

FIG. 6. LAY-OUT OF HANDLEBAR CONTROLS ON THE 1954–60 O.H.V. MODEL LH ("COLT")

Note that unlike the other Ariel singles, the "Colt" has no exhaust-valve lifter, air lever, or ignition lever. The 1955 model shown has a detachable ignition key (withdrawn) in the centre of the combined ignition and lighting switch. On 1956–8 "Colts" plastic ignition and lighting switches are mounted separately on the near- and off-sides of the headlamp shell respectively. 1957–60 headlamps contain an ammeter on the headlamp casing

Now raise the exhaust-valve lifter, and with the instep of the right foot firmly on the kick-starter crank rubber, kick down the starter smartly to its full extent. Release the exhaust-valve lifter when the kick-starter crank is *half-way* down. The engine should fire instantly, or at least on second kick. As soon as it fires, advance the ignition lever *fully* and open the air lever *half to three-quarters* open, opening it fully within about *half a minute*. A moderately fast tick-over speed is desirable. Too slow a speed induces low-temperature condensation, and an excessive speed is likely to overheat the engine, both undesirable conditions, especially for a new engine.

Never permit an air-cooled motor-cycle engine to tick-over, with the motor-cycle stationary, for more than a few minutes. Note that, provided there is sufficient suitable engine oil in the tank, the dry-sump lubrication system always functions automatically. To satisfy yourself that the system is functioning correctly, remove the oil tank filler cap and check that oil is flowing regularly from the orifice of the oil-return pipe. On 1939–50 models having an instrument panel (*see* Fig. 5) instead of removing the filler cap you can check whether the oil gauge at the rear of the instrument panel is indicating a normal tick-over pressure (normally about 5 lb per sq in.).

Kick-starting (All 1954–60 200 c.c. "Colts"). The small cylinder-capacity Model LH has a handlebar control lay-out (*see* Fig. 6) of much simpler type than that specified on the other singles. Starting up is thus extremely easy after setting the controls as described on page 9. To obtain a quick start it is merely necessary to kick down the starter smartly and fully once, or at most twice, when the engine should fire. No subsequent control adjustment is necessary, but it is perhaps desirable to confirm proper oil circulation at the oil-return pipe orifice in the oil tank.

Difficulty in Starting. A tendency for an Ariel engine (except a "Colt" engine) to back-fire while attempting to start up generally indicates that the ignition lever has been excessively advanced. The remedy is obvious.

Quick starting is an acquired knack which comes with experience. If the engine refuses to start, repeat the starting procedure several times, but do not flood the carburettor each time. Once should be quite sufficient. Exact setting of the engine controls is the most important point. If the engine fails to start after half a dozen attempts, kick it over several times with the exhaust-valve lifter raised or plug removed (on a "Colt"), so as to clear what is probably an excessively rich mixture. If the engine still refuses to respond, consult the Table on page 12, and take the appropriate action. The diagnosis of engine trouble is best effected by a process of elimination. Even experts usually adopt this method.

Table I, by the way, applies also to 1954–60 200 c.c. "Colt" engines with coil ignition, but here (referring to the left- to right-hand groups) there is to consider: no ignition lever, carburettor air-slide, exhaust-valve lifter, or valves.

On "Colt" engines erratic running can be caused by a faulty ignition switch which causes a short-circuit. On all engines do not forget to check whether the petrol tank filler-cap vent is choked; this can cause a fuel shortage, and consequent erratic running.

Oil Pressure Readings (1939–50 Models). The oil pressure gauge housed at the rear of the instrument panel, mounted on the petrol tank, records oil pressure readings varying from 5 lb per sq in. (with engine ticking-over) to 10–15 lb per sq in. (while riding). The exact pressure indicated is *not important*, but some pressure should be indicated by the needle to prove that the oil circulation is normal.

TABLE I

CAUSES OF MINOR AND MAJOR ENGINE TROUBLE ("MAGDYNO" MODELS)

Poor or No Spark at Plug	Incorrect Mixture	Weak Compression	Oil Supply Insufficient	Condition of Engine Bad
Incorrect plug gap	Choked jets or incorrectly adjusted jet	Small tappet or rocker clearance	Loose oil pipe connexion	Heavy carbon deposits
Plug insulation dirty or oily		Exhaust valve held off its seat by lifter lever	Ball valve in oil pump not seating	Broken or weak valve springs
Unsuitable type of sparking plug	Incorrect size of main jet		Choked filters or oil pipe	Badly worn valves and valve guides
Faulty plug insulation	Flooding by badly seating needle	Valves not seating due to badly worn guides	Poor joint between timing case and pump face	Incorrect valve timing due to wear of cam levers
Retarded ignition				
Damaged H.T. lead	Faulty condition of engine control wires	Valves require to be ground-in		
Fault in "Magdyno" contact-breaker, or condenser	Faulty adjustment of taper needle	Excessive ring gaps	Incorrectly fitted pump face joint washer	Badly worn bearings
H.T. brush worn or seized in holder	Worn needle-jet, or worn slides	Stuck or broken rings	Broken oil delivery pipe to mainshaft	Clearances reduced due to engine seizure
	Punctured carb. float	Defective cylinder head joint	Tank needs replenishing	Worn cylinder and piston
	Air leak at flange joint of carburettor	Badly scored piston or cylinder		Worn or damaged rings
				Distortion by overheating

CHANGING GEAR

Ease the Ariel off its stand, with the engine ticking over and the foot gear-change pedal of the Burman gearbox in neutral, sit astride the machine, and disengage the clutch, using the handlebar lever (*see* Figs. 3–6).

Low Gear (Changing Up to First). Raise the foot gear-change pedal *fully* with the toe of the foot and engage first (bottom) gear (*see* Figs. 7 and 8). Slight backward or forward movement of the machine often facilitates engagement. As soon as first gear is *felt* to engage, remove the toe from the pedal.

If difficulty is experienced in engaging first gear, wait a few seconds before making another attempt. Initial difficulty in engaging first gear on a *new* machine usually cures itself quite soon, and sticking clutch plates can be rectified by stopping the engine with the exhaust-valve lifter or ignition switch (on "Colts"), and smartly operating the kick-starter several times with the clutch fully disengaged.

Moving Off on the Road. Having engaged first gear, move off by slowly releasing the clutch lever. As the machine gathers speed and the engine takes the full load, gradually increase the throttle opening by means of the

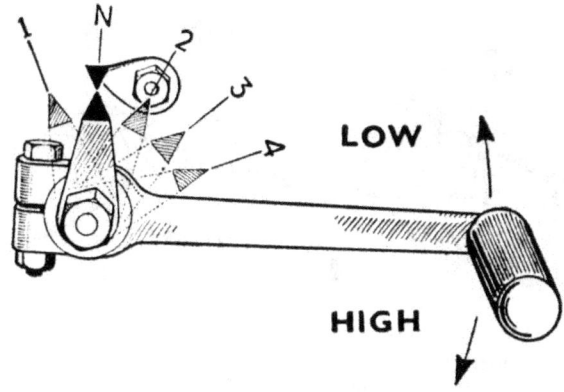

Fig. 7. The Foot Gear-change Indicator (1939–52 Models)

All changes up to a higher gear are made by *depressing* the pedal with the toe, and all changes down to a lower gear by *raising* the pedal with the toe. Internal springs return the pedal to the horizontal position after each gear change is made

twist-grip, so as to maintain a progressive rise in the speed of the engine and machine.

To Change Up (First to Second). As soon as your Ariel has reached a speed of about twelve m.p.h. in first gear, change up into second gear. Once again disengage the clutch, slightly close the throttle, pause a second (halfway between the gears) and then *depress* the gear-change pedal to its *full extent* with the toe, until second gear is *felt* to engage perfectly. Then engage the clutch and also remove the toe from the pedal to allow the pedal to return to its normal position.

High Gears (Changing Up to Third and Fourth). Progressively increase the throttle opening until about twenty m.p.h. is obtained. Now disengage the clutch, throttle down slightly, pause a second, and then smartly, but without force, *depress* the gear-change pedal fully until third gear is *felt* to engage perfectly. Engage the clutch, remove the toe from the pedal, and throttle up to maintain a good road speed without any tendency for the engine to "knock." To change into fourth (i.e. top gear) repeat the procedure at approximately twenty-five m.p.h.

Changing Down (Fourth to Third). Throttle down to a normal speed for third gear. Disengage the clutch, throttle up slightly, pause a second, and *raise* the gear-change pedal quickly to its *full extent* with the toe of the foot until third gear is *felt* to engage. During the change allow the clutch to slip. Immediately afterwards engage the clutch, remove the toe from the

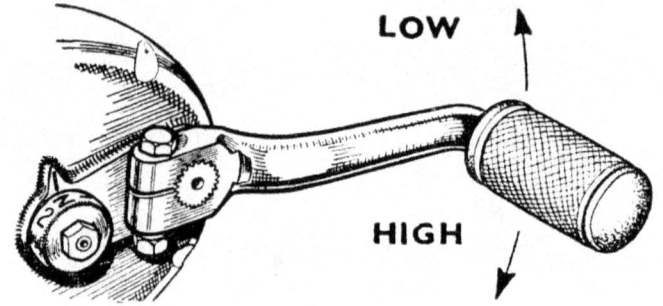

FIG. 8. THE FOOT GEAR-CHANGE INDICATOR (1953–60 MODELS)

The indicator itself comprises a small drum having the gear positions marked as shown. *N* (neutral) is shown aligned with the dash mark on the gearbox shell

pedal, and throttle up to compensate for the increase in the speed of the engine relative to rear wheel speed.

Low Gears (Changing Down to Second and First). The required procedure is similar to that just described for changing down from fourth to third gear. With the toe of the foot *raise* the gear-change pedal to its *full extent* during each gear change. Each full movement of the pedal engages the *next* gear in the gear-change sequence as shown by the indicator in Figs. 7 and 8.

To change from fourth or third gear into first (bottom) gear, it is not *essential* to complete the full gear-changing procedure for each intermediate gear, although this should be done when hill climbing. The method which can be used is to bring the machine to a crawl by means of the throttle and brakes, disengage the clutch, and then raise the gear-change pedal to its *full extent*—three times or twice (in quick succession), according to whether top or third gear was previously engaged. Each time you raise the gear-change pedal "blip" the engine, i.e. throttle up slightly. Then gently re-engage the clutch.

Learn to Change Gear Well. Noisy and poor gear changing are bad for sensitive ears, and worse still for the gearbox! Here are a few golden rules—

1. Make full use of the four gear ratios provided. The gear-change pedal always returns to the same position, but do not forget where it is.
2. Do not "bully" the machine up a steep incline in top gear.
3. Change gear *before* your mount gets "hot and bothered."
4. Use a nicely co-ordinated and almost simultaneous movement when operating the clutch, throttle, and gear-change pedal.
5. Keep a steady pressure on the gear-change pedal and hold the clutch out *until the gear is felt to engage.* At other times remove the foot.
6. Do not race the engine in the lower gears to "impress the lads." They may like it (perhaps) but your engine will hate you!
7. Do not stay in gear for long with the clutch disengaged and the motor-cycle stationary. Instead engage "neutral."
8. Be kind to the gearbox and give it its oil ration occasionally (*see* page 69).

Tackling Hills. Your Ariel will romp up moderate gradients, but maintain the engine revolutions high by making full and intelligent use of the Burman gearbox, where desirable, and *in good time.* On no account allow the engine to labour. Be liberal with the opening of the throttle, and do not retard the ignition lever (omitted on "Colts") unless slight retarding is called for (to eliminate knocking), as late ignition timing necessarily reduces the power output of the engine.

When cruising down steep hills on a "Magdyno" model, open the air lever wide. Besides cooling the engine, this enables engine compression to be utilized as a powerful brake, with no effort on your part.

Good Braking. Always acquire the habit of using *both* brakes simultaneously, as this increases braking power to the maximum, with minimum and even wear of the brake linings and tyres.

Do not forget that sudden and excessive brake application is apt to cause undue wear of the transmission and tyres. Therefore always cultivate the habit of *driving on the throttle;* use the brakes as little and as seldom as possible. As advised in a previous paragraph, utilize engine compression as a brake when descending steep hills on a "Magdyno" model. Never use the exhaust-valve lifter or the clutch for controlling the speed of your Ariel.

Halting the Machine. To effect a normal stop on the road, use the procedure given below—
1. Close the throttle twist-grip completely.
2. Disengage the clutch fully.
3. Apply both brakes together, increasing the foot and hand pressure as the brakes come into action.
4. Raise the foot gear-change pedal fully once or several times (according to which gear is being disengaged) until you get into first (bottom)

gear. Then apply a slight *downward* movement of the gear-change pedal with the toe until "neutral" (*see* Figs. 7 and 8) is obtained. The amount of downward movement normally required is about *half a stroke*. Should any difficulty in obtaining "neutral" be encountered, suspect a dragging clutch.

5. Engage the clutch by gently releasing the handlebar lever.

Stopping the Engine. After bringing a "Magdyno" model to a complete halt with the throttle closed as far as the throttle-stop setting* permits, it is only necessary to raise the exhaust-valve lifter (except on 200 c.c. "Colts") for a few seconds to stop the engine. On a 200 c.c. "Colt" switch off the ignition. Before you leave your Ariel turn off the petrol tap to prevent accidental "flooding." On a 1954–5 "Colt" remove the ignition key for the benefit of the battery and to prevent the risk of theft. (*See* also page 17.)

Running-in Is Vital. Until you cover 1,000 miles it is harmful to accelerate quickly or indulge in excessive speed where a new or reconditioned Ariel is concerned. Refrain from using full throttle until 1,000–1,500 miles have been covered, but *progressively* increase the throttle openings after covering 1,000 miles. A new or reconditioned engine must never be subjected to excessive friction and heat, and unless it is properly run-in a deterioration rather than an increase in performance may occur; in certain circumstances the engine may suffer permanent damage. Here are some good running-in tips—

1. Do not exceed *half* full throttle on "Magdyno" models until you have covered 1,000 miles, and always step up the speed *gradually* and progressively. On the 200 c.c. Ariel "Colt" do not exceed 30 m.p.h. for 500 miles, 40 m.p.h. for the next 250 miles, and do not use full throttle until 1,000 miles have been covered; then use it only for *very* brief periods.

2. Do not run the engine at an excessive speed when idling or on the road, especially in the low gears, and do not "blip" the engine unnecessarily.

3. Avoid exceeding 30 m.p.h. in top gear during the first 1,000 miles wherever possible. Some increase in speed is not harmful towards the end of the running-in period, provided that an excessive throttle opening is not given.

4. Never allow the engine to labour or "knock." Change down in good time, especially where a sidecar outfit is concerned.

5. Never run the engine with the machine stationary for more than a minute or two.

6. Always remember to keep the engine, gearbox and machine correctly

---

* The correct throttle-stop setting is such that when the engine is warmed up and the throttle twist-grip is closed, the engine ticks over smoothly (*see* page 10).

lubricated (see Chapter IV). It is advisable to change the engine oil at 250, 500, and 1,000 miles while running-in.

It is beneficial during the running-in period to mix *one pint* of Acheson's Colloidal Graphite with each *gallon of engine oil*. This benefits the cylinder and bearing surfaces. If the compound (obtainable from most garages) is used after running-in, reduce the amount by one-half. Alternatively use upper-cylinder lubricant (e.g. "Redex") which can to advantage be mixed with the petrol throughout the life of the engine.

Bedding-down While Running-in. A certain amount of bedding-down occurs while running-in, and it is important to check the adjustment of the following: (*a*) tappets or overhead rockers, (*b*) contact-breaker points, (*c*) steering-head bearings, (*d*) primary and secondary chains, and (*e*) brakes. Steering-head bearing adjustment is very important, as slack bearings will suffer. After the initial bedding-down and necessary adjustments have been made, further adjustment is needed much less frequently. During running-in (especially at 250 and 500 miles) check over all bolts, nuts, and screws for tightness. Some are sure to slacken off. Pay special attention to those on the engine and its close vicinity.

The Steering-head Lock. All 1956 and later S.V. and O.H.V. standard-type Ariel singles have a steering-head lock which is a press fit in the base of the steering-head lug and secured by a small grub-screw. To operate this excellent thief-proof device when parking an Ariel, insert the Yale key into the key-hole (see Fig. 9) and turn the key when the steering is moved over to the *left or right* to nearly its full extent. Be careful not to lose the key; for safety, keep it on your key-ring.

If the steering-head lock has been exposed to severe weather conditions, stiffness can be eliminated by applying a few drops of *very thin machine oil* to the *outer* edge of the moving cylinder, but never attempt to lubricate the *inside* of the locking device, which on assembly is packed thoroughly with a special lubricant.

If You Lose Yale Keys. Two Yale keys are provided with each steering-head lock, and the accidental loss of both keys is most unlikely, but nevertheless possible. Note that spare keys can be obtained from any Ariel dealer, provided that you first specify the *code number* of the locking device. The code number is stamped upon the lock barrel, but it is invisible until the lock is withdrawn from the steering-head lug by removing the small grub-screw and prising the lock downwards.

Use of Steering Damper. For sidecar driving and high-speed solo work, especially on rough roads, make full use of the steering damper. But do not tighten the steering excessively by turning the damper knob too far in a clockwise direction; slacken off the damper while reducing speed, as stiff steering at low speeds is unpleasant and sometimes dangerous.

Attaching a Sidecar. Note that stronger telescopic front-fork springs are required for a sidecar outfit than for a solo model. If you attach a sidecar to an Ariel bought for solo use, take the motor-cycle to an Ariel

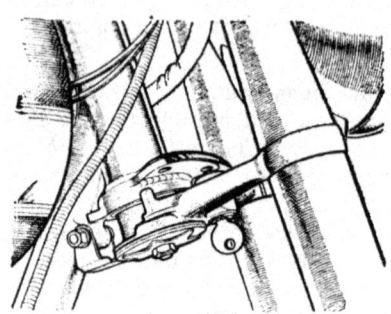

FIG. 9. THE 1956–60 STEERING-HEAD LOCK WITH YALE KEY INSERTED
(*By courtesy of "Motor Cycle," London*)

dealer and get him to fit heavy-duty springs to the telescopic front-forks. Do not attempt to fit the springs yourself.

Sound Advice on Riding. Always wear a good crash-helmet for protection against careless car drivers. Watch out intently for lady car drivers with "L" plates up; give them a wide berth. Always give correct hand-signals, and give them *in good time*. Keep your speed well down in built-up areas where all kinds of peculiar things happen! Avoid excessive noise (especially near hospitals), and always ride in a state of constantly expecting the unexpected. To sum up, always ride with due consideration for all other road users (animals included), and conform with the law in both letter and spirit. Live and let live!

CHAPTER II

CORRECT CARBURATION

A STANDARD type Amal needle-jet carburettor is provided on all 1939–54 single-cylinder 200 c.c., 250 c.c., 350 c.c., 500 c.c., and 600 c.c. Ariel engines, but all 1955 and later engines have the "Monobloc" type Amal needle-jet carburettor fitted.

STANDARD TYPE AMAL CARBURETTOR

Functioning. Some knowledge of the working of the standard type of Amal carburettor is recommended, as this assists tuning and maintenance. Referring to Fig. 10, showing a sectional view of the Amal semi-automatic carburettor, (A) is the carburettor body or mixing chamber, the upper part of which has a throttle valve (B), with taper needle (C) attached by a needle clip. The throttle valve regulates the quantity of mixture supplied to the engine. Passing through the throttle valve (except on the 1954 200 c.c. "Colt" engine) is the air valve (D), independently operated and serving the purpose of obstructing the main air-passage for starting and mixture regulation. Fixed to the underside of the mixing chamber by the union nut (E) is the jet block (F), and interposed between them is a fibre washer to ensure a good petrol-tight joint.

On the upper part of the jet block is the adaptor body (H) forming a clean through-way. Integral with the jet block is the pilot jet (J), supplied through the pilot feed-hole (K). The adjustable pilot air-intake (L) communicates with a chamber, from which issues the pilot outlet (M) and the by-pass (N). A throttle-stop (*see* Fig. 11) is provided on the mixing chamber, by which the position of the throttle valve for tick-over is regulated independently of the cable adjustment.

The needle jet (O) is screwed in the underside of the jet block and carries at its bottom end the main jet (P). Both these jets are removable when the jet plug (Q), which bolts the mixing chamber and the float chamber together, is removed. The float chamber, which has bottom feed, consists of the chamber (R) fed with petrol through union (S). It contains the float (T) and the float-needle valve (U) attached by the clip (V). The float-chamber cover (W) has a lock screw (X) for security.

The petrol tap having been turned on, petrol will flow past the float needle-valve (U) until the quantity of petrol in the chamber (R) is sufficient to raise the float T, when the needle valve (U) will prevent a further supply entering the float chamber until some in the chamber has already been used up by the engine. The float chamber having filled to its correct level,

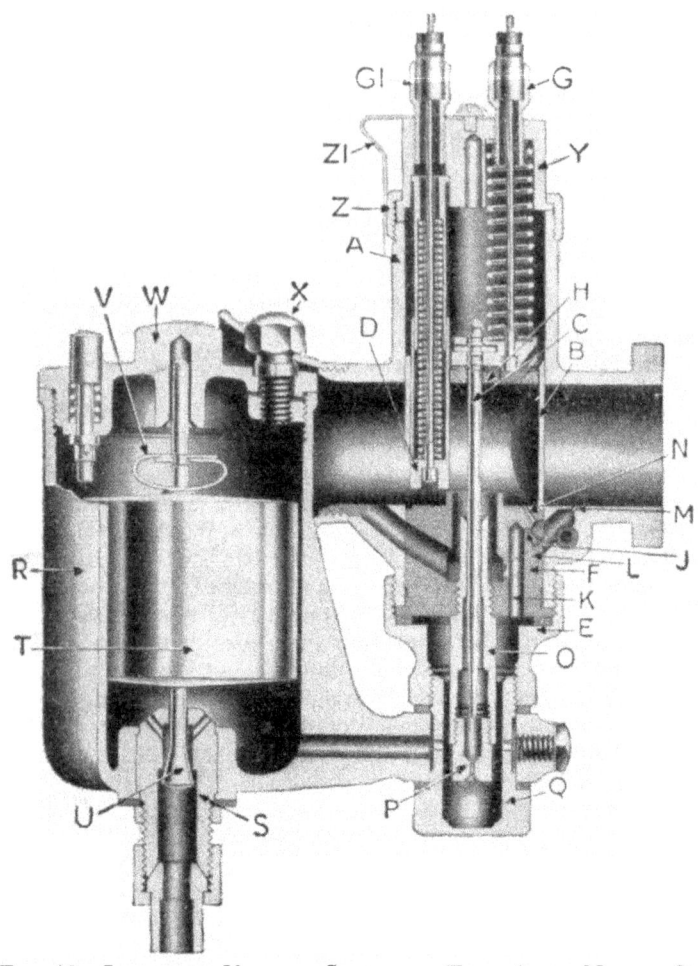

FIG. 10. SECTIONAL VIEW OF STANDARD TYPE AMAL NEEDLE JET CARBURETTOR FITTED TO 1939–54 MODELS

On the 1954 200 c.c. O.H.V. Model LH ("Colt") the air valve (D) and the cable and adjuster (G1) are omitted

A = Mixing chamber
B = Throttle valve
C = Jet needle and clip
D = Air valve
E = Mixing-chamber union nut
F = Jet block
G = Cable adjuster for throttle valve
G1 = Cable adjuster for air valve
H = Adaptor body
J = Pilot jet (integral)
K = Pilot feed-hole
L = Pilot air-intake
M = Pilot outlet
N = Pilot by-pass

O = Needle jet
P = Main jet
Q = Jet plug
R = Float chamber
S = Union for float chamber
T = Float
U = Float-needle valve
V = Float-needle clip
W = Float-chamber cover
X = Float-chamber lock screw
Y = Mixing-chamber cap
Z = Lock-ring for Y
Z1 = Locking spring

the fuel passes along the passages through the diagonal holes in the jet plug (Q), when it will be in communication with the main jet (P) and the pilot feed-hole (K); the level in the needle and pilot jets is, obviously, the same as that maintained in the float chamber.

Imagine the throttle valve (B) very slightly open. As the piston descends, a partial vacuum is created in the carburettor, causing a rush of air through the pilot air-intake (L), and drawing fuel from the pilot jet (J). The mixture of air and fuel is admitted to the engine through the pilot outlet (M). The quantity of mixture capable of being passed by the pilot outlet M is insufficient to run the engine. This mixture also carries excess of fuel. Consequently, before a combustible mixture is admitted, the throttle valve B must be slightly raised, admitting a further supply of air from the main air-intake.

The farther the throttle valve is opened, the less will be the depression on the outlet (M) but, in turn, a higher depression will be created on the pilot by-pass (N), and the pilot mixture will flow from this passage as well as from the pilot outlet (M).

The mixture supplied by the pilot and by-pass system is supplemented at about one-eighth throttle by fuel from the main jet (P), the throttle valve cut-away determining the mixture strength from here to one-quarter throttle. Proceeding up the throttle range, mixture control by the needle position occurs from one-quarter to three-quarters throttle, and from this point the main jet is the only regulation.

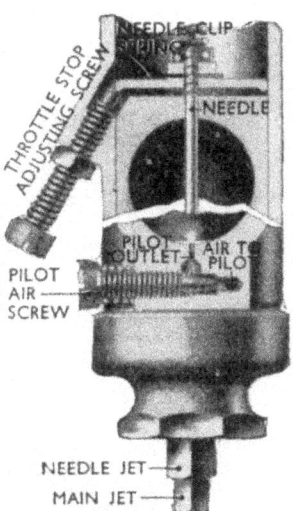

Fig. 11. Throttle-stop and Pilot-air Adjusting Screws (Standard Carburettor)

For the arrangement of the "monobloc" instrument, see Fig. 12

The air valve (D), which is cable-operated, has the effect of obstructing the main through-way and, in consequence, increasing the depression on the main jet, enriching the mixture. Two cable adjusters (G), ($G1$) are provided to take up cable stretch.

"MONOBLOC" TYPE AMAL CARBURETTOR

Functioning. The "Monobloc" type Amal carburettor, fitted to all 1955 and later Ariel engines, differs from the standard type of instrument used on S.V. and O.H.V. singles prior to 1955 in several fairly important respects, but its general functioning is similar. The "Monobloc" design includes: a horizontal float chamber made integral with the carburettor body; a float needle of moulded nylon; a top petrol-feed; a needle jet

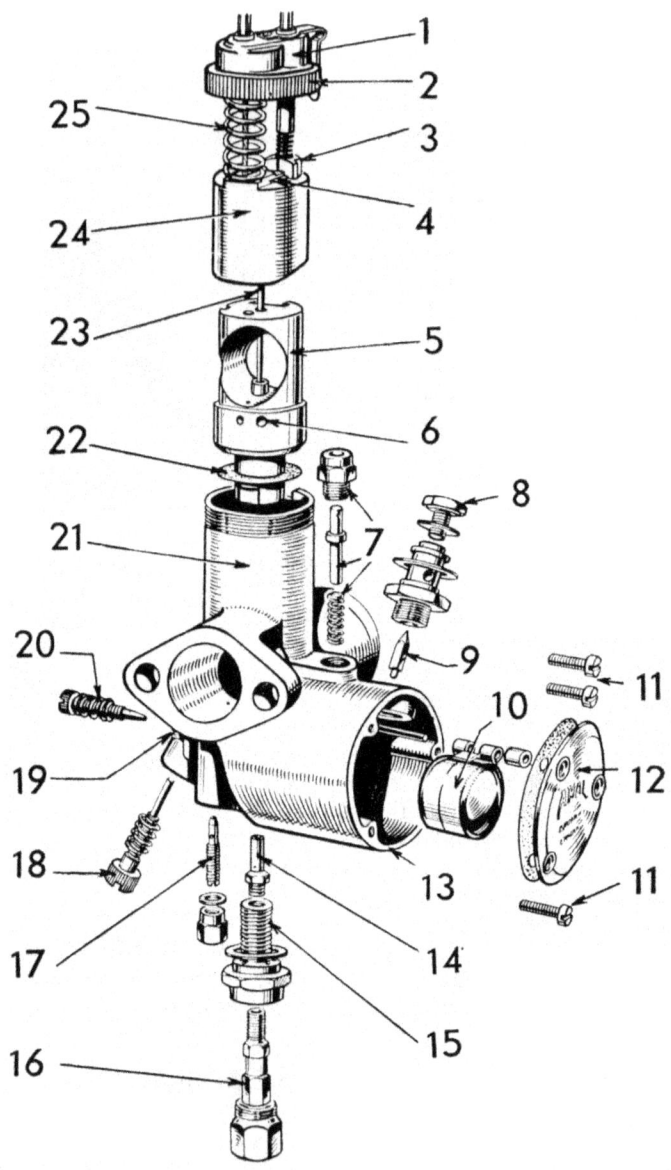

Fig 12. Exploded View of Amal "Monobloc" Type Carburettor (1955 Onwards)

with bleed holes giving two-way compensation; and a detachable pilot jet which can be easily cleaned.

Fig. 12 illustrates the essential parts of the instrument. The float chamber (13) and float needle (9) maintain a constant level of petrol in the needle-jet (14) and the pilot jet (17). The selection by the makers of the appropriate jet sizes and main-bore choke ensures a proper atomizing and proportioning of the petrol and air sucked into the engine.

The air valve (3) is normally kept fully raised, and the throttle valve (24), controlled by the handlebar twist-grip, regulates the volume of mixture, and therefore the power. At all throttle openings a correct mixture is automatically obtained.

The "Monobloc" type carburettor, like the standard type instrument, operates in four stages. When opening the throttle from the fully closed position to one-eighth open (for tick-over) the mixture is supplied by the pilot jet (17), and the strength of the mixture is determined by the setting of the knurled pilot air-adjusting screw (20) which has a coil locking-spring to facilitate adjustment. As the throttle is opened slightly farther, the main jet system comes into action, the mixture being augmented by the main jet (16) through the pilot by-pass.

The amount of cut-away on the atmospheric side of the throttle valve regulates the petrol-to-air ratio between one-eighth and one-quarter throttle. The needle jet (14) and the jet needle (23) take over the mixture regulation between one-quarter and three-quarter throttle, and the mixture strength is determined by the relative position of the needle in the clip (4) attached to the throttle valve (24). When the throttle is opened beyond three-quarters, the mixture strength is determined only by the size of the main jet. Note that the main jet (16) does not spray petrol direct into the carburettor mixing chamber, but discharges through the needle jet into the primary air chamber. From there it enters the main choke through the primary air choke. The latter has a two-way compensating action in conjunction with the "bleed" holes in the needle jet. Pilot and main jet behaviour are not affected by this two-way compensation which governs only acceleration at normal cruising speed.

KEY TO FIG. 12

1. Mixing-chamber cap
2. Mixing-chamber cap ring
3. Air valve
4. Jet-needle clip
5. Jet block
6. Air passage to pilot jet
7. Tickler assembly
8. Banjo securing-bolt
9. Float needle
10. Float
11. Float-chamber cover screws
12. Float-chamber cover
13. Float chamber
14. Needle jet
15. Main-jet holder
16. Main jet
17. Pilot jet
18. Throttle-stop adjusting screw
19. Jet block locating-screw
20. Pilot air-adjusting screw
21. Mixing chamber
22. Fibre seal
23. Jet needle
24. Throttle valve
25. Throttle return-spring

TUNING THE CARBURETTOR (STANDARD AND "MONOBLOC" TYPE AMAL)

The same tuning instructions apply to the standard and "Monobloc" type instruments. Normally it is unwise to interfere with the maker's carburettor setting (*see* Table II) unless there is a very special reason for doing so. However, it is sometimes desirable to make a slow-running adjustment with the pilot adjusting screw.

To obtain good slow-running, observe the instructions below.

To vary the strength of the normal running mixture, it is necessary to adjust the height of the needle in the throttle valve, or else to fit a larger or smaller size main jet. The condition of the sparking plug provides an excellent guide to the condition of the mixture.

Slow-running Adjustment. This should be effected with the engine already warmed up. If the adjustment is appreciably at fault, screw home the pilot air-adjusting screw fully and then unscrew it (usually about two complete turns) until the engine idles at an excessive speed, with the throttle twist-grip closed and the throttle slide abutting the throttle-stop screw. The air lever should be fully open and the ignition lever (where automatic

TABLE II
AMAL CARBURETTOR SETTINGS FOR 1939–60 ARIEL MODELS

Ariel Model	Main Jet Size	Throttle Valve	Needle Position*
OG, OH (1939–49)	110	5/3	3
VA (1939–49)	140	6/4	3
VG (1939–49)	170	6/4	3
VG (1950)	160	6/4	3
NG (1939–50)	110	5/4	3
NH (1939–54)	150	6/4	3
NH (1955–60)	200	$3\frac{1}{2}$	3
VH (1939–51)	200	29/4	3
VH, VHA (1952–4)	200	29/3	3
VH (1955–60)	200	$3\frac{1}{2}$	3
VB (1939–49)	160	6/5	3
VB (1950–54)	160	6/4	3
VB (1955–8)	220	5	3
LH (1954)	75	5/3	3
LH (1955)	90	$3\frac{1}{2}$	3
LH (1956–60)	110	$3\frac{1}{2}$	3

* Note that needle position 3 means the third notch from the top.

ignition-advance is not provided) should be set to obtain the best slow-running (half to two-thirds advanced).

Loosen the nut (omitted on the "Monobloc" type carburettor) securing the throttle-stop screw, and unscrew the latter until the engine slows up and begins to falter. Then screw the pilot air-adjusting screw in or out as required to enable the engine to run regularly and faster. To weaken the mixture, screw the pilot air-adjusting screw *outwards*.

Next gently lower the throttle-stop screw until the engine again begins to falter. Now lock the throttle-stop screw with the lock-nut (omitted on "Monobloc" type carburettor) and begin to readjust the pilot air-adjusting screw to obtain the optimum slow-running. Should this second adjustment cause the engine to tick-over at an excessive speed, repeat the adjustment a third time.

It is important to avoid excessive richness of the slow-running mixture, especially if much riding is done on small throttle openings; if the mixture is too rich, considerable running on the pilot jet will occur while riding, with consequently a high fuel consumption.

Aim at obtaining the best tick-over on a mixture bordering on the weak side. The engine should be on the point of spitting-back. When perfect slow-running* has been obtained, tighten the lock-nut (standard type carburettor) on the throttle-stop screw without disturbing the position of the screw.

Altering Jet-needle Position. The tapered jet needle secured by a clip to the throttle valve regulates the mixture between about *one-quarter and three-quarter full throttle*. The tapered jet needle and the needle jet gradually wear, through continuous movement of the throttle, and this slowly enriches the mixture within the throttle range just referred to, thereby increasing the petrol consumption. The remedy is to lower the tapered jet needle *one notch* by securing it in No. 2 position or, in the event of bad wear existing, in No. 1 position. If an excessively rich mixture persists after lowering the jet needle so that it is in the top notch, renew both the jet needle and the needle jet. The size of the main jet (below the needle jet) determines the mixture strength from *three-quarter to full throttle*.

Bad Slow-running. If it is found impossible to obtain good slow-running by making the pilot air adjustment as described on page 24, it is possible that there are air leaks, due to a poor joint at the carburettor attachment to the cylinder and/or a worn inlet-valve guide. Badly seating valves will

---

* Rev the engine up and down sharply several times and note whether the exhaust is nice and crisp, with no "flat spots" as the twist-grip is rotated. It is essential to obtain good acceleration as well as good tick-over. When making this test, the ignition lever (where fitted) must be *fully advanced*. Never run the engine fast with the ignition lever even slightly retarded.

also weaken the mixture. Defects in the ignition system may also be responsible for poor tick-over. The sparking plug may be oily, or the points set too close (*see* page 81). Possibly the spark is excessively advanced or the contact-breaker needs attention (*see* page 83). See that the H.T. pick-up brush on "Magdyno" models is bedding down and in good condition; also that the slip-ring is clean. Examine the H.T. cable for signs of shorting.

Pilot-Jet Obstructed. If the pilot-jet adjustment does not obtain the desired results and the engine will not idle nicely with the throttle almost closed, the air lever wide open, and the ignition (if manual control is provided) half to two-thirds advanced, it is possible that the pilot jet is obstructed. The jet on the standard type carburettor is actually a duct drilled in the jet block, is very small, and can readily become choked.

To obtain access to the pilot jet on the standard type carburettor, remove the jet plug and float chamber (*see* Fig. 10), and detach the jet block by pushing or tapping it out of the carburettor body. The pilot jet can then be cleared by blowing. On the "Monobloc" type carburettor it is only necessary to remove the cover nut below the pilot jet (17) shown in Fig. 12, and unscrew the pilot jet.

MAINTENANCE HINTS (1939-59)

Dismantling Standard Type Carburettor. Periodic cleaning is necessary to maintain efficient functioning of the instrument. It is best to disconnect the petrol pipe and then remove the carburettor from the face of the inlet port after unscrewing the carburettor-flange nuts. Referring to Fig. 10, unscrew the mixing-chamber cap lock-ring (*Z*), held by spring (*Z*1); detach the mixing-chamber cap (*Y*). Then pull out the air valve (*D*), omitted on the 1954 "Colt," and the throttle valve (*B*), with the jet needle (*C*) attached. To inspect the two valves, or slides, and the jet needle, it is not *necessary* to detach the two slides from the control cables.

Should you desire to detach the air valve (*D*) from the control cable (*G*1), compress the spring and release the nipple from the base of the slide. To remove the throttle valve (*B*) from the control cable (*G*), compress the spring and permit the cable nipple to vacate the hole in which it seats. Then release the spring and allow the nipple to pass through the larger-sized hole.

In order to remove the taper jet needle (*C*) from the drum-shaped throttle slide, remove the spring clip which is located at the top of the slide. The normal position for the jet needle is given in Table II. Raising or lowering the needle enriches or weakens the mixture respectively.

Next take the float chamber (*R*) off the carburettor. Remove the jet plug (*Q*) from the union nut (*E*). Be careful not to lose either of the two fibre washers (one above and one below the float-chamber lug). Unscrew the lock-screw (*X*) and turn the float-chamber cap (*W*) until this can be removed from the float chamber. To remove the float itself, compress the spring clip (*V*) and withdraw the float (*T*) from the float chamber. On removing the float from the float chamber, the needle (*U*) will come away from the bottom. Take care not to mislay the two fibre washers (one above and one below the float-chamber lug union).

Now remove the needle jet (*O*), thereby exposing the main jet (*P*). Afterwards remove the main jet from the needle jet. Finally unscrew the mixing-chamber union nut *E* and detach the jet block *F*. Should this be stiff, tap it out gently, using a wooden stump inside the mixing chamber.

Dismantling "Monobloc" Type Carburettor. Close the two-level petrol tap and disconnect the petrol pipe by undoing the banjo bolt (8) over the float chamber (*see* Fig. 12). Referring to Fig. 12, unscrew the mixing-chamber knurled cap-ring (2) on top of the carburettor and also remove the two nuts securing the carburettor flange to the face of the inlet port. Then remove the body of the carburettor (21), complete with the integral float chamber (13). While removing the carburettor, pull the air valve (3), omitted on "Colt" engines, and the throttle valve (24) from the mixing chamber and tie them up temporarily out of the way. As mentioned in the instructions for the standard type carburettor, it is rarely necessary to disconnect the slides from the cables. Check that the flange washer is sound.

Further dismantling is straightforward. Referring to Fig. 12, to remove the jet needle (23), withdraw the jet-needle clip (4) on top of the throttle valve, and remove the needle. To obtain access to the float (10), remove the three screws (11) securing the float-chamber cover (12). Lift out the hinged float (10) and withdraw the moulded-nylon needle (9). Lay both aside for cleaning. The float-chamber vent, by the way, is embodied in the tickler assembly (7), and the top-feed union houses a filter element of fine gauze which is readily accessible for cleaning.

To remove the main jet (16), remove the main-jet cover and unscrew the jet from the jet holder (15), which should also be unscrewed. Remove the jet-block locating screw (19) to the left of and slightly below the pilot air-adjusting screw. Then push or tap out the jet block (5) and fibre seal (22) through the large end of the mixing chamber (21). To remove the pilot jet (17), remove the pilot-jet cover nut and unscrew the jet.

Cleaning the Amal Components. Wash all the carburettor components thoroughly clean with petrol and blow through the various ducts and passages to make sure that they are quite clear. Avoid using a fluffy rag for drying purposes. Pay special attention to the small pilot-jet passages in the jet block on both the standard and "Monobloc" type instruments. See that all impurities are removed from inside the float chamber. On the "Monobloc" type carburettor do not forget to clean the detachable pilot jet and the filter gauze inside the top-feed union for the float chamber.

Inspecting Various Parts. When dismantling the carburettor it is advisable to make a close inspection of the various parts if the carburettor has been in continuous service for a considerable period.

1. THE FLOAT CHAMBER. Examine the components very carefully and check that the vent is unobstructed. The float must be in perfect condition. Clean the moulded-nylon needle on the "Monobloc" type carburettor very thoroughly, and be careful not to damage it. On a standard type carburettor hand-polish the valve part of the float needle by rotating the needle on its seat while pulling it vertically upwards. If a distinct shoulder is visible on the needle where it seats, renew the needle at once. Check for any sign of bending or distortion of the clip.

2. THE THROTTLE VALVE. Test this for fit in the mixing chamber. Should excessive play exist, renew the slide forthwith. See that the new slide has the correct amount of cut-away.

3. THE JET-NEEDLE CLIP. The spring clip securing the tapered needle to the throttle valve must grip the needle firmly, and free rotation must *not* occur, as this causes the needle groove to wear. Always be careful to replace the needle with the clip in the correct groove (*see* page 24).

4. THE JET BLOCK. Before tapping this home in the mixing chamber verify by blowing that the pilot-jet ducts are clear and that the jet-block fibre seal is in good condition.

5. THE CARBURETTOR FLANGE. Examine this for truth with a straightedge. Distortion sometimes occurs, and this may cause an air leak. If the flange face is slightly concave, file and rub down the face with emery cloth until it is dead flat and smooth. Alternatively have it faced dead true on a grinder.

Assembling Standard Type Carburettor. Referring to Fig. 10 refit the jet block (F) with the fibre washer on its under side, and screw on lightly the mixing-chamber union nut (E). Screw in the needle jet (O) and the main jet (P). Open the air lever $\frac{7}{8}$ in. (omitted on 1954 "Colt") and the throttle twist-grip half way; grasp the air slide (where fitted) between the thumb and the finger and make sure that the jet needle enters the central hole in the adaptor body (H). Slightly turn the throttle slide until it enters the guide, when on pushing down the slides, the air valve should enter its guide. If not, slightly move the mixing-chamber cap (Y), when the air valve will slide into position. Screw home the mixing-chamber knurled cap-ring (Z). No force is necessary.

Replace the carburettor-flange washer, offer up the carburettor body to the cylinder head, and secure in position by tightening evenly the two nuts. Replace the float and needle in the float chamber, holding the needle against its seating with a pencil until the float (T) and needle clip (V) are slipped into position. See that the spring clip enters the needle groove. Then screw home the float-chamber cover securely and lock in position by tightening the lock-screw (X).

Insert the jet plug (*Q*) in the union nut (*E*) and very firmly tighten the union nut with a suitable spanner. Remove the jet plug and fit the float chamber and secure with the jet plug. Be sure there is a fibre washer above and below the float-chamber lug as shown in Fig. 10. When the float chamber has been correctly positioned, tighten the jet plug firmly. Finally reconnect the petrol pipe and tighten the union nut at the base of the float chamber. In the event of the pilot-jet adjustment having been disturbed, re-tune as described on pages 24–6.

Assembling "Monobloc" Type Carburettor. Do this in the reverse order of dismantling. Referring to Fig. 12, screw home the pilot jet (17) and the pilot-jet cover nut, not omitting to replace its washer. Push or tap home the jet block (5) and fibre seal (22) through the large end of the mixing chamber (21). Check that the fibre-seal fitted to the stub of the jet block is in good condition. Then fit the jet-block locating-screw (19). Screw the main-jet holder (15) into the jet block, after checking that the washer for the holder is sound. Next screw the main jet (16) into the main-jet holder.

Replace the moulded-nylon needle (9) in the float chamber (13), and fit the hinged float (10) with the *narrow* side of the hinge uppermost. Afterwards fit the float-chamber cover (12) and secure by means of the three screws (11). Verify that the cover and body faces are undamaged and quite clean. Renew the washer.

If previously removed, attach the jet needle (23) to the throttle valve (24) and secure with the jet-needle clip (4), making sure that the clip enters the correct groove (*see* Table II on page 24).

Position the carburettor-flange washer, and offer up the carburettor to the face of the inlet port after easing the air (except on 1955–8 "Colts") and throttle valves (3) and (24) down into the mixing chamber (*see* previous hints concerning the standard type carburettor). When easing the throttle valve home, make sure that the tapered jet needle (23) really enters the hole in the jet block (5). Secure the carburettor flange firmly to the engine by means of the two nuts, and tighten these evenly. Tighten down firmly the mixing-chamber knurled cap-ring (2) and see that the throttle slide works freely when this is tightened down.

Finally reconnect the petrol pipe by tightening the banjo securing-bolt (8) over the float chamber (13).

Attention to Air Filter (1954–60). The air filter specified on 1954–60 S.V. and O.H.V. singles has an oil-impregnated gauze element, and some attention is advisable every 1,000–1,500 miles; in dusty and dry areas the lower mileage is recommended. Remove the gauze element, wash in petrol or paraffin, and dry off. Then immerse the element in light engine oil (SAE 20), drain off all surplus oil, and replace the gauze element in the filter casing.

CHAPTER III

THE LIGHTING EQUIPMENT

THIS chapter covers solely the maintenance of the electrical equipment (generators, batteries, and lamps) provided specifically for lighting purposes, though on 1954–60 200 c.c. coil-ignition "Colt" models (models LH) the battery is used for both lighting and ignition. For advice on lubrication, refer to the appropriate section in Chapter IV. Chapter V covers those items responsible for the functioning of the ignition system (i.e., the magneto, contact-breaker, coil, sparking plug, etc.). For instructions on the use of the ignition switch ("Colt" models), *see* Chapter I, page 9.

The Lucas "Magdyno" Dynamo (1939–60). The generator used for charging the Lucas battery on all except the 1954–60 Ariel "Colts" is a Lucas chain-driven "Magdyno" unit comprising a 6-volt detachable dynamo strapped above a face-cam type magneto. Compensated voltage control is standard on all Lucas dynamos and sees to it that the battery is kept charged automatically to the correct amount; the cut-out is mounted independently in a box comprising the C.V.C. unit. Up to about 1945 a Lucas E3HM dynamo was specified. This had a lubricator on the commutator end-bracket, but all later Ariels have a Lucas E3LM dynamo with no lubricator fitted.

DYNAMO MAINTENANCE ("MAGDYNO")

Before interfering with the wiring, always disconnect the battery positive lead* from the switch lead, to avoid the danger of short circuits which might cause serious damage. On 1939–50 models to disconnect, move the rubber shield and unscrew the cable connector; do not touch the frame with the connector and cause a short-circuit. When reconnecting, pull the rubber shield well over the connector. To disconnect the battery lead from a battery with detachable cable-connexions, unscrew the knurled nut and withdraw the collet or cone-shaped insert. Note that the two terminal collets are not interchangeable, so it is impossible to reconnect the wrong lead.

If at any time the motor-cycle must be ridden with the battery disconnected, or in any way out of service, it is possible to run with the switch in any position without damaging the electrical equipment.

---

* On 1951 and later Ariels a "positive earth" system is used, and the battery *negative* lead should be disconnected.

Inspecting Brushgear. It is advisable about every 6,000 miles to remove the metal cover-band from the dynamo and inspect the brushgear and commutator. When removing the cover-band it is not necessary to disconnect either lead from the battery.

See that the dynamo brushes work freely in their holders. This can be easily ascertained by holding back each retaining spring and gently pulling each flexible lead; the brush should move without the slightest sluggishness. It should also return to its original position directly the lead is let

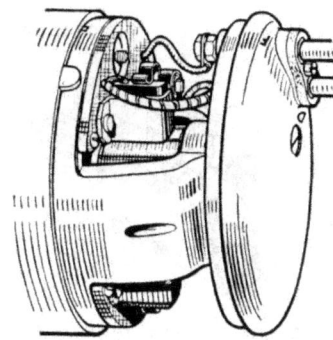

FIG. 13. COMMUTATOR END OF LUCAS E3LM AND E3HM DYNAMO OR DYNAMO PORTION OF THE "MAGDYNO"

Some thin machine oil should be put in the lubricator (E3HM dynamo) about every 2,000–3,000 miles. The driving-end bearing is packed with H.M.P. grease on assembly

go. When testing a brush in this way, release it gently, otherwise it may get chipped. The brushes should be clean and "bed" over the whole surface; that is, the face in contact with the commutator should appear uniformly polished. Dirty or sticking brushes may be cleaned, after removal, with a cloth moistened with petrol Always replace carbon brushes in their original positions and see that they make firm contact with the commutator segments.

If the brushes become badly worn, remove them as follows. Release the eyelet on the brush lead by unscrewing the hexagonal nut or screw at the terminal. Then, holding back the spring lever out of the way, withdraw the brush from its holder. Replace with genuine Lucas brushes.

The brush springs should be inspected occasionally to see that they have sufficient tension to keep the brushes firmly pressed against the commutator when the dynamo is running; keep this in mind when the brushes have been in use a long time and are very much worn down. It is unwise to insert brushes of a grade other than that supplied with the dynamo, or to change the tension springs. When the brushes become so worn that they no longer bed down on the commutator, go to a Lucas service agent.

Keeping Commutator Clean. The surface of the commutator should be kept clean and free from oil or brush dust, etc. Should any grease or oil work its way on to the commutator through over-lubrication, it will cause sparking, and carbon and copper dust will be collected in the grooves between the commutator segments.

The best way to clean the commutator without disconnecting any leads is to remove from its holder one of the main brushes and, inserting a dry duster in the holder, hold it, with a suitably-shaped piece of wood, against the commutator surface, causing the armature to be rotated at the same

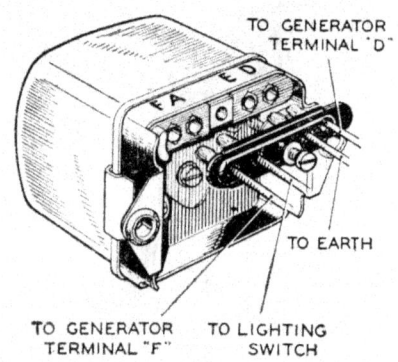

FIG. 14. LUCAS C.V.C. UNIT (1955–60 "MAGDYNO" MODELS) SHOWING THE CONNEXIONS

On earlier models the connexions are in the sequence F, A, D, E, and the two screws are used to hold the connector plate

time. If the commutator has been neglected for a long period, it may need cleaning with fine glasspaper, but care must be taken. The segments should be *dark bronze* and highly polished.

Dynamo Leads and C.V.C. Unit Terminals. On a Lucas "Magdyno" with a separate compensated voltage-control (C.V.C.) unit the dynamo positive terminal is marked "*D*" and the shunt-field terminal "*F*" on the cover. To connect up, first slacken the fixing screw on the terminal block and remove the clamping plate. Then withdraw the metal sleeve from each terminal. The cables should then be passed through the clamping-plate holes and bared at the ends for ⅜ in. Now fit the sleeves over the cables, bend back the wires over them, and push the sleeves home into the terminals, finally screwing down the clamping plate (*see* Fig. 14).

General Servicing. It is a good plan every 10,000 miles to entrust the dynamo to a Lucas service depot for dismantling, cleaning, servicing, and lubrication.

THE LIGHTING EQUIPMENT

Compensated Voltage Control. This is used on all 1939 and later "Magdyno" models. Wiring diagrams are given on pages 44–6. The control unit comprises the cut-out and voltage control (working on the trembler principle) neatly housed in a casing mounted on the rear mudguard beneath the saddle or dualseat. The unit sees to it that the battery is kept properly charged automatically, the dynamo output varying according to the state of charge of the battery and the load.

With C.V.C. equipment the lighting switch is provided with only three positions—*Off*, *L*, and *H* (*see* page 39). In all three positions the dynamo gives a controlled output, thus relieving the rider of much responsibility. The regulator begins to operate when the dynamo voltage reaches about 7·3 volts. During daylight running when the battery is well charged the ammeter may indicate a charge of only 1 or 2 amp, for the dynamo gives only a trickle charge. The cut-out prevents the battery discharging when the dynamo is not charging.

The regulator provides for an increase of dynamo output as soon as the lamps are switched on. The effect of switching the lamps on after a long run with the battery voltage high is often to cause a temporary discharge reading at the ammeter, but fairly soon the voltage falls and the regulator responds, thereby causing the output of the dynamo to balance the load of the lamps.

When the battery is in a discharged state, the regulator increases the dynamo output and restores the battery to its normal state of charge in the shortest possible time.

Note that on "Magdyno" models with C.V.C. unit fitted, it is possible to run with the battery disconnected or removed, and the lamps switched on without incurring any risk of burning out the bulbs. Where the battery is disconnected, the negative lead to it (the positive lead on "negative earth" system) should be taped up, not earthed.

C.V.C. Unit Not Adjustable. The unit is sealed by the makers, and does not need adjustment once it is correctly set. The only conceivable trouble is from the contacts oxidizing or welding together, owing to accidental crossing of the dynamo field and positive leads. Be careful if making wiring alterations (*see* page 43). Referring to Fig. 14 make sure that the C.V.C. unit connexions are correct, tight, and that the insulation is sound.

To Remove and Replace Dynamo. On 1939 and later "Magdyno" models with compensated voltage control, first disconnect the connexions from the dynamo terminals. Unscrew the hexagon nut from the "Magdyno" driving-end cover. Then loosen the two screws which fasten the band clip. The dynamo can then be withdrawn from the rest of the "Magdyno" unit.

On assembling the dynamo, slide it through the band clip so that the fixing screw passes through the hole in the end cover. See that the gears mesh properly. Tighten the end-cover nut and the two band-clip securing screws. Then connect up the connexions to the dynamo terminals. Verify that this is correctly done. Referring to Fig. 14, it will be noted that the cable from the cut-out and regulator terminal (D) is connected to a similarly marked terminal on the dynamo. The same applies to the cut-out and regulator terminal (F).

Fuses Not Specified. In order to simplify the system as far as possible, no fuse is provided. If all the connexions are kept clean and tight, there is no possibility of any excess current causing damage to the equipment.

The Ammeter. This indicates the amount of current flowing into or from the battery and shows whether the battery is being charged or discharged. It is of the centre-zero type and mounted on a headlamp panel or on a fascia.

BATTERY MAINTENANCE (LUCAS)

It is extremely important that the Lucas battery on all "Magdyno" models should receive regular and correct attention. The following are the essential points concerning battery maintenance—

1. Always keep the battery well charged.
2. Top up the cells fortnightly, or at the latest monthly, with distilled water.
3. Keep the electrolyte level with the tops of the separators.
4. Keep the battery and terminals clean, and the terminals tight.
5. If in doubt, check the specific-gravity readings of the electrolyte with a hydrometer.
6. If the battery is not in use, have it charged monthly.

Topping up Battery Cells. Inspect the level of the electrolyte about every two weeks, and more frequently in very hot climates. On all models unscrew and remove the single slotted-bolt or the two sleeve-bolts which clamp the battery to the battery carrier (*see* Fig. 15). Pull aside the hinged metal strap and withdraw the battery. Take off the battery lid and remove the three vent plugs. Inspect the hole in each vent plug and make quite sure that it is not obstructed. A choked vent-plug hole causes an increase in pressure within the battery cell when "gassing" occurs, and may create trouble. Check that the rubber sealing-washer (when fitted) for each vent plug is intact, otherwise leakage of the electrolyte may occur.

Wipe the battery top clean with a rag and afterwards wash the rag thoroughly in water or destroy it. See that a supply of clean distilled water (obtainable from chemists and garages) is available for topping up the cells. The distilled water, unlike the sulphuric acid, gradually evaporates and must be replenished.

With the vent plugs removed, inspect the level of the electrolyte in each

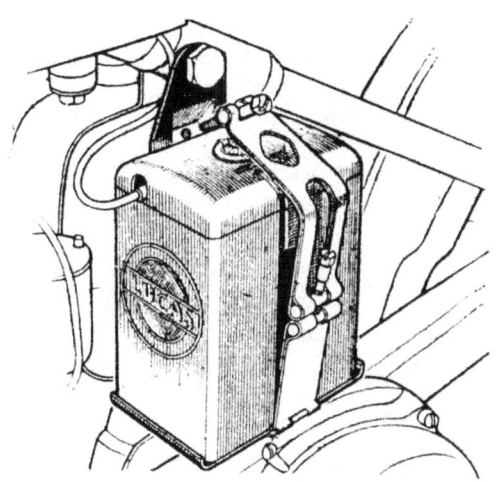

Fig. 15. Battery Clamp with Two-bolt Fixing Partially Removed
(*By courtesy of "Motor Cycle," London*)

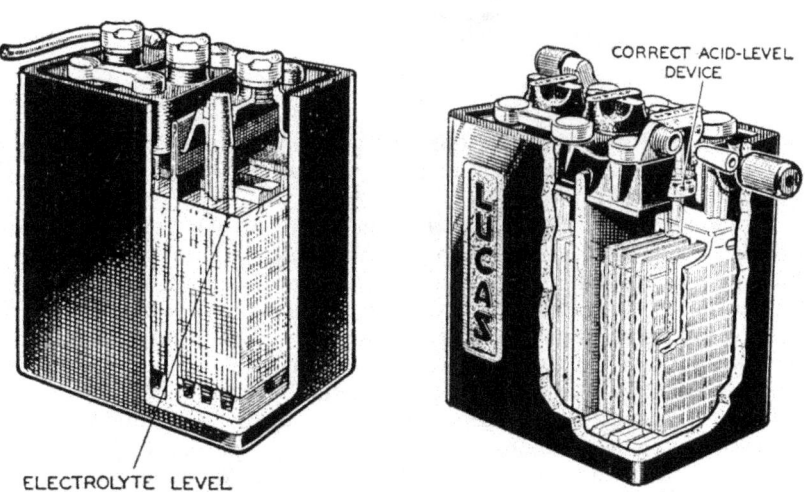

ELECTROLYTE LEVEL

Figs. 16 and 16a. Two Types of Lucas Battery Fitted to Ariel Models

The battery shown on the left is fitted to 1939–53 models and differs rom the battery shown on the right (fitted to most 1954–60 models) in that no acid-level device is used

cell. On no account hold a naked light near the vents. If the level of the electrolyte is below the tops of the separators, add distilled water as required to bring the level correct (*see* Fig. 16). Do this *before* a charge run, as the agitation accompanying charging and "gassing" thoroughly mixes the electrolyte solution.

Where no acid-level device (*see* Fig. 16A) is provided, insert the nozzle of a Lucas battery filler into each cell as shown in Fig. 17 until the nozzle rests

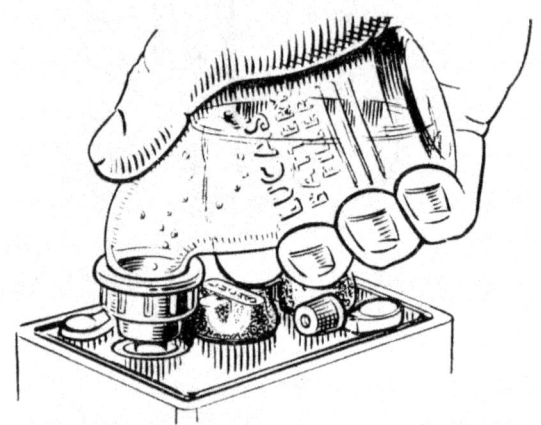

FIG. 17. TOPPING-UP A CELL WITH THE LUCAS BATTERY FILLER

on the separators. Hold the filler in this position until air bubbles stop rising in the glass container. The cell is then topped up to the correct level (shown in Fig. 16).

To top up a Lucas battery of later type having an acid-level device, pour distilled water round its flange (not down the tube) until no more drains through into the cell. This occurs when the level of the electrolyte reaches the bottom of the central tube and prevents further escape of air displaced by the topping-up water. Lift the tube slightly to permit the small quantity of water in the flange to drain into the cell; the level of the electrolyte will then be correct. Alternatively use the method just described.

Do not add acid to the electrolyte unless some of the solution has been accidentally spilled. In this case add diluted sulphuric acid of specific gravity equal to that in the cells. Finally replace the vent plugs, fit the battery, and strap it down securely. See that the battery leads are firmly and correctly re-connected.

Using Lucas Battery Filler. When replenishing the Lucas battery filler with distilled water, see that the screw-on nozzle is replaced correctly. Be sure that the rubber washer is fitted over the valve with the small peg in the centre of the valve engaging the hole in the projecting boss of the washer.

The Battery Connexions. Always keep the connexions clean, free from corrosion, and tight, otherwise the ammeter readings will *not* indicate the true state of charge of the battery. To prevent corrosion, smear the connexions with petroleum jelly.

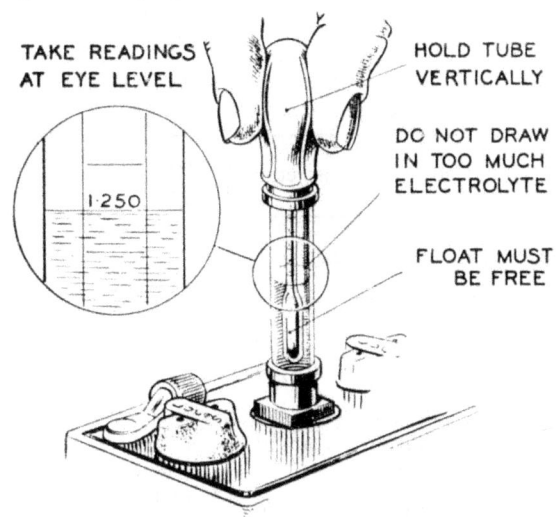

FIG. 18. CHECKING THE SPECIFIC GRAVITY OF THE ELECTROLYTE WITH A LUCAS HYDROMETER

Checking Battery Condition. If any loss of acid has occurred, the battery is misbehaving, or its condition is suspect, it is advisable to check the battery condition by taking specific gravity readings (with a hydrometer) of the electrolyte in each cell. Fig. 18 indicates the correct method of doing this. Note that it is not advisable to take S.G. readings immediately after topping up the battery, as the electrolyte will not then be properly mixed. The Lucas hydrometer shown resembles a syringe containing a graduated float which indicates the specific gravity of the electrolyte in the battery cell from which a sample is taken.

When checking the S.G. of the electrolyte in each cell, note that the spaces between the separators are not wide enough to allow the hydrometer nozzle to be inserted. Therefore, before taking a sample, tilt the battery to bring sufficient electrolyte above the separators. After a sample has been taken and checked, it must, of course, be returned to the appropriate cell. Taking S.G. readings with a hydrometer is the most efficient way of determining the state of charge of the battery and its general condition.

The specific gravity readings (*see* Tables III and IV) should be approximately the *same for all three cells*. If the reading for one cell varies substantially from the readings for the other two cells, probably some acid has been spilled, or has leaked from the cell concerned. A short-circuit between the battery plates is also a possibility to be considered. If such a short exists, return the battery immediately to a Lucas service depot for expert attention.

TABLE III

Specific Gravity Readings for Lucas Batteries
(Temperature below 90° F)

Lighting System	Cell Fully Charged	About Half Discharged	Fully Discharged
"Magdyno"	1·270–1·290	1·190–1·210	1·110–1·130

TABLE IV

Specific Gravity Readings for Lucas Batteries
(Temperature above 90° F)

Lighting System	Cell Fully Charged	About Half Discharged	Fully Discharged
"Magdyno"	1·210–1·230	1·130–1·150	1·050–1·070

Note that a low state of charge of the battery is often caused by parking the machine for long periods with the pilot light and rear lamp switched on, unaccompanied by much daylight running. The remedy is, of course, to undertake more daylight running until the battery regains its normal state of charge. Should over-charging occur, get the compensated voltage control unit checked at a Lucas service depot.

Storage of Battery. If the equipment is laid by for several months, the battery must be given a small charge from a separate source of electrical energy about once a month, in order to prevent any permanent sulphation of the plates. In no circumstances must the electrolyte be removed from the battery and the plates allowed to dry, as certain chemical changes take place which result in permanent loss of capacity.

THE LIGHTING EQUIPMENT 39

HINTS ON LUCAS LAMPS

Lucas lamps are designed to provide maximum illumination with the minimum of attention, and few instructions are necessary with regard to the maintenance of this part of the electrical equipment.

Three Lighting-Switch Positions. Compensated voltage control is provided on all 1939 and later Ariel "Magdyno" models, and therefore the dynamo charges the battery when the engine is running with the lighting switch in any of its three positions which are as follows—

Off: Headlamp, tail lamp, speedometer, and sidecar lamp (where fitted) switched off.

L: Headlamp pilot bulb, tail lamp, speedometer, and sidecar lamp (where fitted) on.

H: Headlamp main bulb, tail lamp, speedometer, and sidecar lamp (where fitted) on.

Correct Headlamp Alignment. If the headlamp is incorrectly aligned and/or the main bulb is out of focus, maximum road illumination will not be obtained, and other road users may be inconvenienced by dazzle. It is easy to rectify both faults.

The best method of checking the alignment of the headlamp is to stand your Ariel facing a light-coloured wall at a distance of approximately 25–30 feet. Switch on the main driving light and note if the beam is projected straight ahead and parallel with the ground.

Take vertical measurements from the centre of the headlamp, and from the centre of the illuminated circle on the wall, to the ground. Both measurements should be equal. If they are unequal, loosen the two fixing bolts securing the headlamp in the front-fork mounting brackets and tilt the headlamp until the centre of the beam is truly parallel with the ground. Afterwards tighten the two fixing bolts firmly.

Focusing and Non-Focusing Headlamps. On all new Ariels the double-filament main bulb is carefully focused to give the best illumination. Provided that Lucas bulbs of the correct wattage and number are fitted as replacements, subsequent re-focusing should not be necessary, unless the focusing adjustment has been disturbed. 1952–60 models with the Lucas SS700P, SSU700P/1 or MCH16 headlamp have a main bulb which is permanently "pre-focused."

Narrowly converging and widely diverging beams are highly undesirable as they illuminate the road poorly and are liable to dazzle other road users. Adjust the focus of the headlamp immediately if its *beam* is not uniform, is too wide, is of short range, or has a dark centre. To focus the headlamp (where a focusing adjustment is provided) it is necessary to remove the lamp front and then slacken the screw on the bulb holder clamping clip as illustrated in Fig. 20. The bulb holder can then be moved backwards or

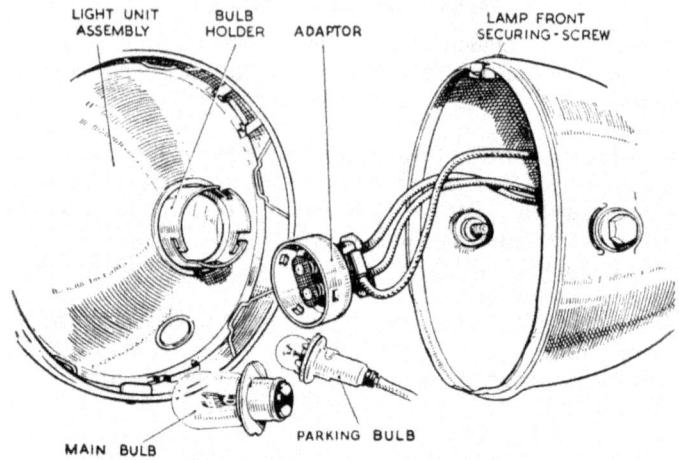

Fig. 19. Typical Lucas Headlamp with Light-unit Assembly and "Pre-focus" Main Bulb

There are several variations of the parking bulb arrangement with this type of headlamp, introduced about 1954, but in all instances there is no focusing adjustment for the flanged main bulb, and the reflector and lens are a unit

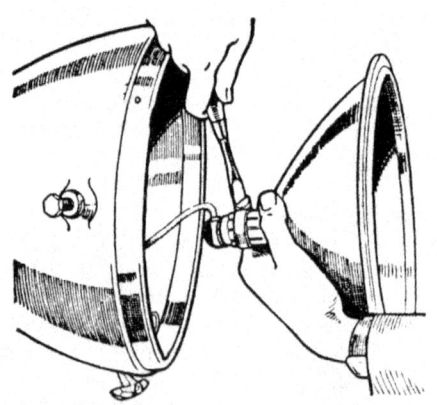

Fig. 20. Slackening the Bulb Holder Clamping-clip on Typical Focusing-type Lucas Headlamp

A focusing-type headlamp is fitted to most 1939–53 Ariels

forwards on the reflector axis until the headlamp is focused correctly. Focus the headlamp against a light-coloured wall approximately 25–30 feet away from the headlamp. See that the bulb holder clamping-screw is firmly re-tightened after making a final adjustment. For correct bulb renewals, *see* below.

Cleaning Lucas Lamps. The reflector is most important. Never scratch its surface during handling, and avoid finger-marking the surface, readily done on Lucas DU142, and MU42 headlamps.

Never clean the reflector with metal polish. Lucas reflectors have a colourless and transparent protective covering. To clean any finger marks (except on Lucas light-units), polish the surface gently with a chamois leather or with a clean, *very soft* dry cloth such as a Selvyt.

Clean the black surfaces of the lamp body with a good car polish, and polish the chromium-plated rim with a chamois leather or a soft, dry cloth, after first washing off any dirt with water.

LUCAS BULB RENEWAL

When fitting a new bulb to a Lucas headlamp, see that the bulb is of Lucas manufacture. Lucas bulbs are specially designed for use with Lucas reflectors; another make of bulb may *not* always give the best results.

Where a double-filament main (focusing-type) bulb is concerned, it is important to make sure that the bulb is fitted with the dipped-beam filament *above* the centre filament. After fitting a new main bulb it is sometimes desirable to check the focus of the headlamp (*see* page 39).

Bulbs for 1939–49 Lamps. For the 1939–49 Lucas DU142 and MU42 type headlamps, and the Lucas tail lamps, the correct bulb renewals are—

Main bulb: 6-volt, 24-watt, double-filament, Lucas No. 168.
Pilot (also instrument panel, where fitted) bulb: 6-volt, 3-watt, Lucas No. 200.
Tail-lamp bulb: 6-volt, 6-watt, Lucas No. 205.

Bulbs for 1950–1 Lamps. For 1950–1 "Magdyno" models, with the Lucas focusing-type (52053) headlamp, the correct bulb renewals are as follows—

Main bulb: 6-volt, 30/30-watt, double-filament, Lucas No. 169.
Pilot bulb: 6-volt, 3-watt, Lucas No. 200.
Tail-lamp bulb: 6-volt, 6-watt, Lucas No. 205.

Bulbs for 1952–60 Lamps. For all 1952–9 "Magdyno" models having the Lucas SSU700P, SSU700P/1, or MCH16 type headlamp specified (with "pre-focus" main bulb), the correct bulb renewals are as follows—

Main bulb: 6-volt, 30/24 watt, double-filament, Lucas No. 312.
Pilot bulb: 6-volt, 3-watt, Lucas No. 988.

Tail lamp bulb: 6-volt, 6-watt, Lucas No. 205.
Stop-tail lamp bulb (where fitted): 6-volt, 6/18-watt, Lucas No. 383.

No. 169 and 312 Bulbs. When renewing the No. 169 main bulb, always replace it correctly in the SSU700P focusing-type headlamp. To assist correct replacement, the metal cap is marked "TOP." The bulb holder is secured in position by two spring-loaded pegs and can readily be removed from the rear of the Lucas light-unit after detaching the lamp front and light-unit assembly.

Some 1950–1 type 52053 and all 1954–6 SSU700P/1 headlamps with underslung pilot light are of the "pre-focus" type (Fig. 19) with no focusing adjustment, and require a No. 312 main bulb.

The No. 312 "pre-focus" bulb can be readily identified, as it has a broad locating flange on its cap. It can be fitted in its holder in one position only, and cannot be fitted to a focusing type SSU700P headlamp. Referring to Fig. 19, to replace a "pre-focus" bulb, turn the adaptor *anti-clockwise*, pull it off, and remove the bulb from the holder in the rear of the reflector. Fit the new bulb (No. 312) in the holder, engage the projections on the inside of the adaptor with the slots in the bulb holder, press on the shell, and secure by turning clockwise. This applies also to the 1957–60 MCH516 cowled headlamp.

If the underslung pilot-bulb of a 1954–6 Lucas SSU700P/1 "pre-focus" headlamp requires renewing, slide out the metal carrier-plate above the pilot lens, and fit the new bulb (No. 988). See that the plate is pressed firmly home afterwards, or it may work free while riding and cause the pilot light to go out, possibly unnoticed by the rider. Those who dislike underslung pilot-lights are well catered for by various proprietary makes of "dual-lights," which can be readily fitted, one on each side of the headlamp.

Bulb Renewal on Cowled Headlamps (1956–60). To obtain access to a "pre-focus" main or pilot bulb, remove the headlamp front after partially releasing the fixing screw at the base of the lamp rim. Before doing this, however, it is necessary to withdraw the Lucas headlamp forward from the cowl (*see* Fig. 21) in the following manner.

Unscrew the headlamp securing-pin (*C*) on each side of the cowl. The inside distance-piece (*B*) falls away, and you can then withdraw the complete headlamp by placing one hand beneath the lamp body and pulling it forward clear of the cowl.

The pilot bulb on the 1957–60 MCH516 headlamp is positioned in the reflector unit by a sprung holder which can readily be pulled out. The "pre-focus" (No. 312) main bulb has a bayonet-type fixing cap and, as previously mentioned, cannot be wrongly inserted. When replacing the headlamp in the cowl be careful first to position each distance piece (*B*) before inserting the screw (*C*).

THE LIGHTING EQUIPMENT

WIRING OF LUCAS EQUIPMENT

Before making any alteration to the wiring, or removing the lighting switch from the back of the Lucas headlamp, disconnect the positive lead (negative lead with positive-earth system) at the battery to prevent the possibility of short circuits. For wiring see Figs. 22–24.

All cables to the headlamp are taken directly into the switch, which can

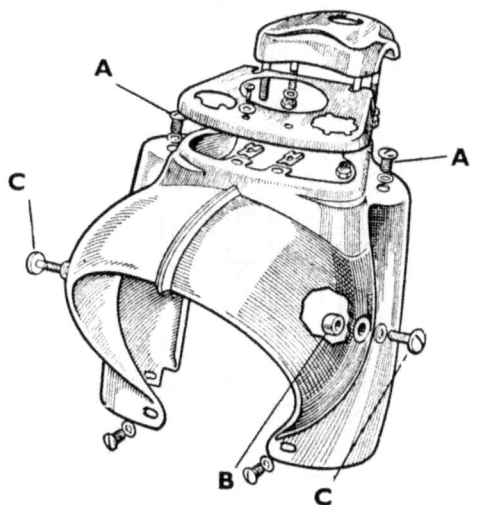

Fig. 21. Details of Headlamp Cowl on 1956–60 "Magdyno" Models

    A. Screw-type plugs for tops of fork legs
    B. Inside distance-piece
    C. Headlamp securing-pins

be easily withdrawn from the lamp body when the fixing screws are removed (pre-1956 models without a cowl).

The various lighting cables are identified by means of coloured sleeves, or by colours on the harness. When making a connexion, proceed as follows: bare about $\frac{3}{8}$ in. of the cable, twist the wire strands together, and turn back about $\frac{1}{8}$ in., so as to form a small ball. Remove the grub-screw from the appropriate terminal and insert the wire so that the ball fits in the terminal post. Now replace and tighten the grub-screw; this will compress the ball to make a good electrical connexion. See that the rubber sleeves are pulled well over the various connectors.

"Factory Exchange" Units. If the harness leads are kept properly clipped or taped to prevent chafing, and the leads are kept free from oil and grease, the wiring harness should last for years without attention. It is desirable, however, about every 15,000 miles (or during a complete overhaul) to remove the dynamo or "Magdyno" and submit it to a Lucas service depot for overhaul, lubrication, and an endurance test for condition. If its general condition has deteriorated, you can exchange the faulty unit for a factory-reconditioned unit. The same applies to the compensated voltage control unit.

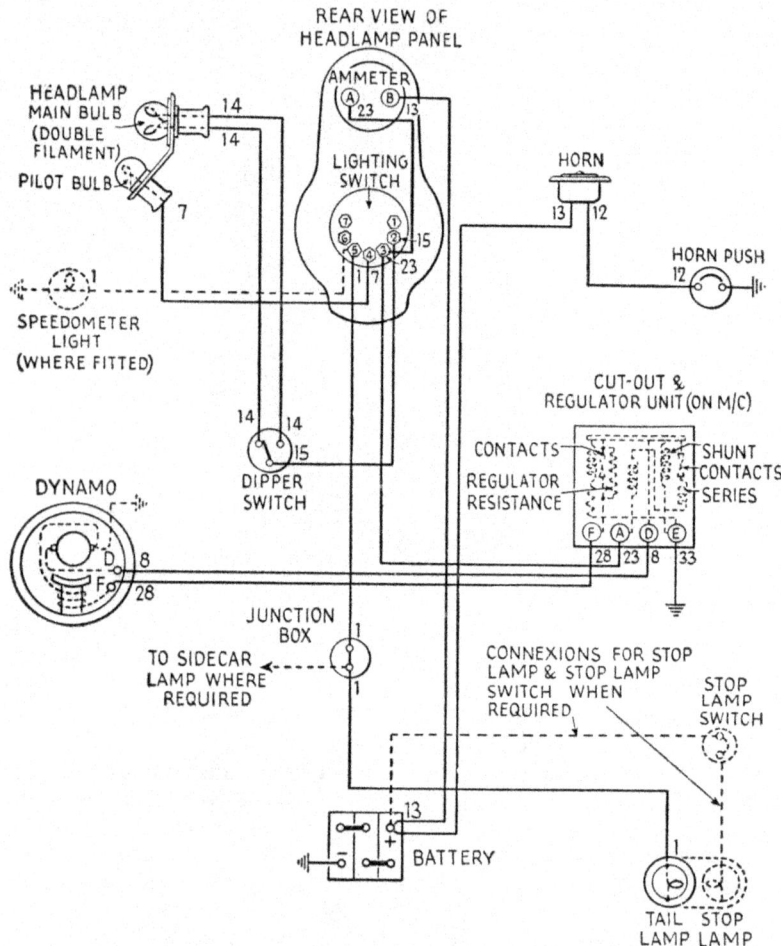

Fig. 22. Wiring Diagram for Lucas "Magdyno" Lighting Equipment (1939–50 Models)

Applies to machines having a "negative earth" system, and a Lucas DU42, MU42, or SSU700P headlamp

KEY TO CABLE COLOURS

1. Red. 7. Red and black. 8. Yellow. 12. Yellow and purple. 13. Yellow and black. 14. Blue. 15. Blue and white. 23. White and purple. 28. Green and black. 33. Black

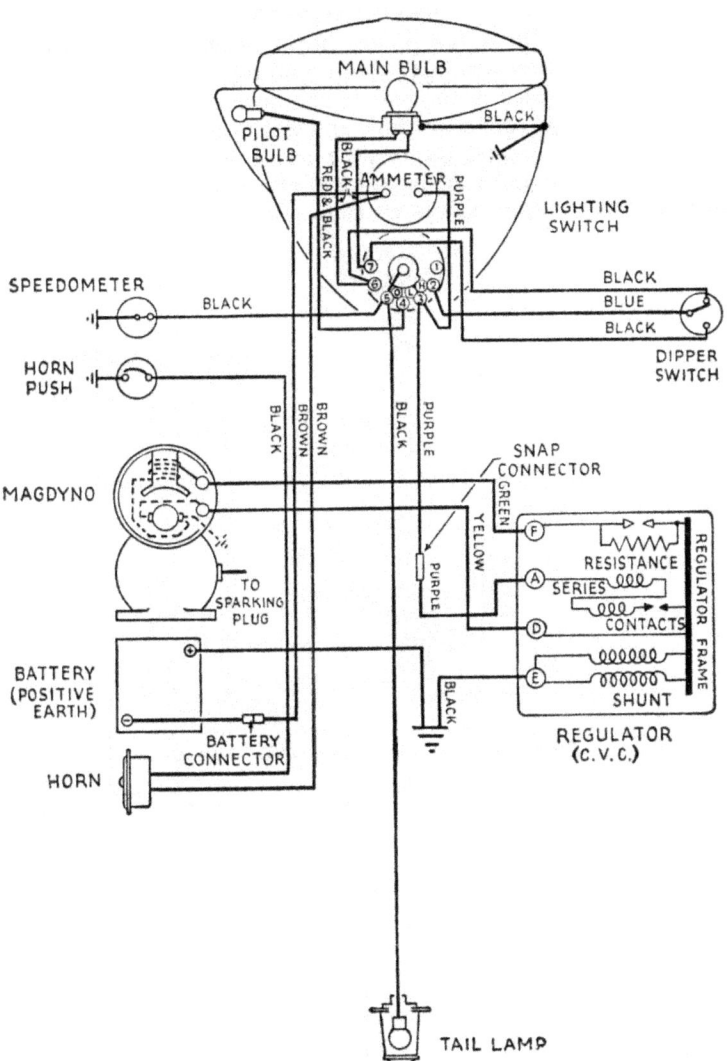

Fig. 23. Wiring Diagram for Lucas "Magdyno" Lighting Equipment (1951–2) Models

Applies to 1951–2 machines having a "positive earth" system and a Lucas SSU700P/1 headlamp. Should a stop-tail lamp be fitted, the lead for the stop-light filament should be connected to the battery negative terminal (with brake switch interposed)

LUCAS HORNS

Tone Adjustment. On a few Lucas horns produced during 1950–1 no tone-adjustment screw was fitted, but on all other Lucas horns an adjustment screw is provided at the rear of the horn. If the performance of a horn deteriorates (roughness of tone and loss of power) the following tone adjustment can be effected. Depress the horn-push and turn the adjustment screw *anti-clockwise* until the horn just fails to sound. Release the horn-push and turn the adjustment screw *clockwise* for six notches (i.e. a quarter

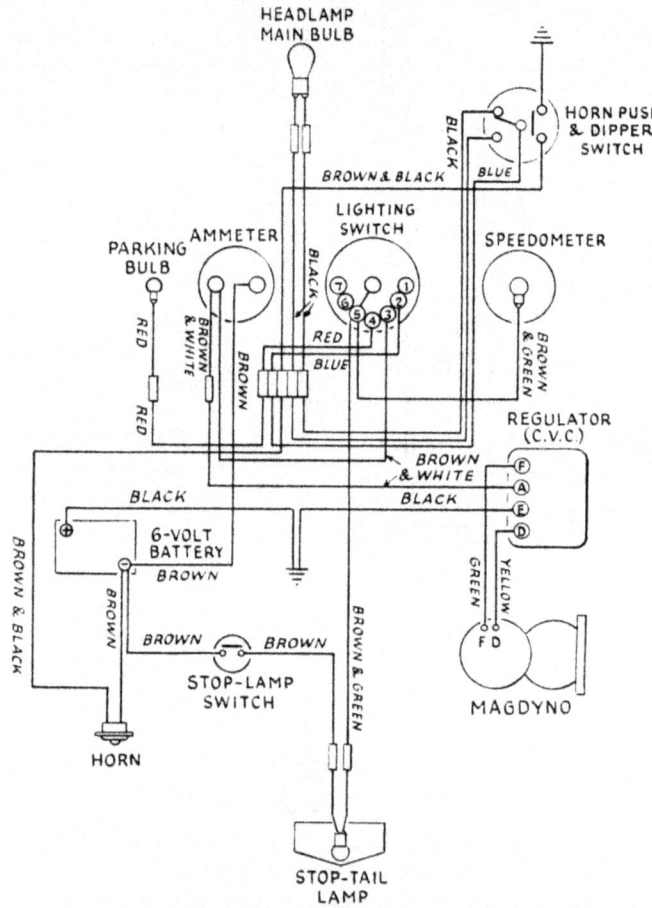

FIG. 24. WIRING DIAGRAM FOR LUCAS "MAGDYNO" LIGHTING EQUIPMENT (1953–60 MODELS)

Applies to 1953–8 Ariels having a "positive earth" system a Lucas SSU700P/1 headlamp, and a stop-tail lamp

of a turn), when the original performance of the horn should be restored, assuming no serious fault exists. If further adjustment is needed, turn the screw *clockwise* one notch at a time.

LIGHTING EQUIPMENT (WIPAC)

On 1954–60 "Colts." The equipment includes a permanent-magnet alternator which charges a battery via a full-wave bridge rectifier. The electrical components (lamps, horn and ignition coil) are connected to the battery. It is the function of the alternator and rectifier to maintain the battery in a charged state for *all load conditions*. This is effected by a system of coil switching, which adjusts the generator output according to the load. The coil design also ensures regulation of the output over the working speed range.

In addition, an "emergency start" facility is provided, whereby the machine may be started if either the battery is flat or the rectifier faulty, or even in the unlikely event of the battery and rectifier both being out of order.

Should only the battery be flat, the emergency start conditon (*see* page 5) will also give a charge into the battery as soon as the machine is running. The individual circuit components are mentioned briefly below.

The Wipac Alternator. The rotor (*see* Fig. 25) comprises six high-grade cast anisotropic magnets with laminated pole pieces. It is self-keeping and may be removed from the stator without any loss of magnetism.

If for any reason it is desired to remove the rotor, which is that part of the alternator attached to the driving side engine mainshaft, it is necessary first to take off the primary chain-case outer cover complete, which is secured by sixteen screws and two bolts. Note very carefully the position of the rear brake pedal adjusting cam which is located in the lower edge of the chain cover. Before the outer chain-case can be withdrawn the adjusting cam must be rotated to the lowest position to ensure clearance.

Next straighten the tab washer and remove the large crankshaft nut, when the rotor can be withdrawn from the keyed parallel driving shaft.

The laminated stator (the stationary coil assembly) has six salient poles, each of which is wound with a coil of enamelled copper wire. These coils are vacuum-impregnated with a special varnish to make them resistant to harmful effects of heat, oil, and petrol. The stator coil assembly is secured by four nuts. Note the position of the aluminium housing and the brass shield protecting the alternator from the ingress of foreign matter.

The Rectifier. This unit is of the full-wave bridge type with selenium plates. It is mounted in a position that ensures air cooling when the machine is moving. *It is essential not to obstruct the air flow to the rectifier* by the fitting of any additional accessories or stowing personal belongings under the saddle or dualseat.

Provided that the leads are securely attached to the rectifier *no service or adjustment should be required*, and in the unlikely event of any trouble occurring with this component, it should be returned complete to the nearest Ariel or Wipac agent.

The Varley Battery (1954–5 "Colts"). The Varley battery is a modified MC 5/9, with 6-volts 10-ampere-hours capacity. It is of the "dry" type and therefore is unspillable. It is, however, necessary to keep the plates

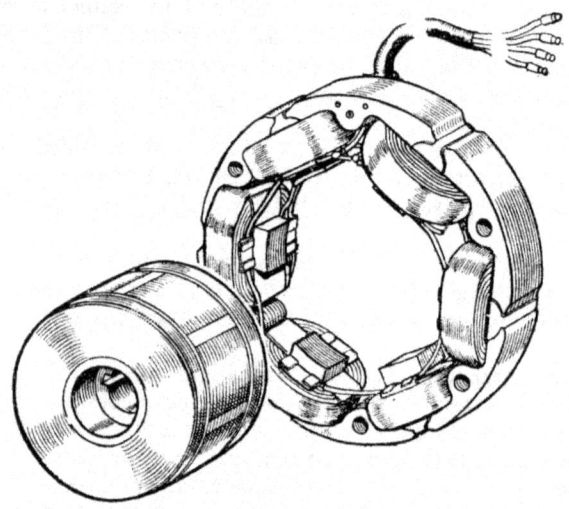

Fig. 25. The Wipac Series 114 Alternating-current Generator
(*By courtesy of "Motor Cycle" London*)

and separators in a moist condition; therefore once a month add a teaspoonful of distilled water to each cell.

After allowing a Varley battery to stand for 15 minutes, any surplus water showing at the top of the battery should be removed with a suitable hydrometer.

The following voltages indicate the approximate state of charge of a Varley battery—

    5·7 volts or under—Fully discharged.
    6·15 volts or under—Partially discharged.
    6·3 volts or over—Open-circuit, fully charged.
    7·8 volts or over—On charge, fully charged.

Do Not Reverse Battery Leads. The *positive* terminal of the battery must always be connected to earth. Note that reversal of the battery leads is likely to cause serious damage to the equipment.

THE LIGHTING EQUIPMENT

Note that in the event of continuous running being undertaken without the battery being used, the battery must be fully disconnected and the *negative* lead connected to an earthed point on the frame of the Ariel "Colt." The detachable ignition key or the plastic ignition switch (1956–9) must also be turned to the "EMG" position.

The Exide Battery (1956–60 "Colts"). Keep the type 3LFT2 battery and surrounding parts, especially the tops of the cells, clean and dry. Also see that the battery terminals and connexions are free from corrosion; it is advisable to smear them with some petroleum jelly. Do not use grease for this purpose. Maintain the vent plugs tightly in position, and never permit the acid level to fall below the tops of the separators. Add distilled water regularly to each cell until the level is $\frac{1}{8}$ in. above the tops of the separators. On no account add acid to the cells.

The amount of charge received by the battery should be sufficient to maintain the specific gravity of the acid in each cell within the limits 1·230 and 1·260. If the specific gravity falls below about 1·150 the battery should be removed from the motor-cycle and given a "bench" charge. Too little charging is indicated by the specific gravity of the acid being frequently below 1·230, and excessive charging by its being generally at the fully-charged value of 1·270 to 1·285. In the latter instance frequent topping up (say weekly) is necessary. If abnormal specific gravity readings persist, consult a battery expert.

A "Bench" Charge. Idle Exide batteries, and also Varley batteries, should receive a "bench" charge about *once a month*. As soon as a battery has reached a fully-charged condition, it should be taken off charge.

In the case of an Exide battery give it a bench charge at 1 ampere until the specific gravity of the acid has shown no rise over a period of 5 hours and all cells are gassing freely and evenly. At this point the specific gravity of the acid should lie between 1·270 and 1·285.

Correct Headlamp Bulbs. The correct bulbs to fit in the Wipac headlamp are—

Main bulb—6-volt, 30/30-watt (twin filament); 30/24-watt pre-focus (1956–9).
Pilot bulb—6-volt, 3-watt.

Renewing Headlamp Bulbs. It is simple to fit new bulbs in the Wipac headlamp. First remove the front rim units by releasing the slotted screw under the headlamp. Then withdraw the old bulbs without disturbing the reflector. Bend back the small locking-tab securing the bulb-holder bracket, and turn the bracket *anti-clockwise*. The main and/or pilot bulb can now be withdrawn. When renewing the main bulb, always see that the dip filament (the one off-set from the centre) is uppermost. The pilot bulb is located below the main bulb.

Headlamp Maintenance. Very little maintenance is necessary. Occasionally see that the multiple wiring connectors are gripping the leads tightly. Keep the headlamp glass nice and clean; a brilliant beam is quickly spoiled by a dirty front glass. At intervals check the securing bolts at the sides of the lamp body for tightness. If the alignment of the headlamp is poor (*see* page 39), loosen the securing bolts and move the headlamp as required.

Wipac Rear Lamps. The correct bulbs to fit are—

Rear lamp bulb—6-volt, 6-watt.
Stop-tail lamp bulb—6-volt, 3-watt.

The 1954–5 stop-tail lamp (*see* Fig. 26) with round body has a red plastic glass, giving a brilliant glow in all directions. It uses a single bulb with twin filaments, but should this be replaced by the later type of lamp with three separate bulbs (*see* Fig. 27), the above-mentioned bulb ratings are also correct. To remove the portion of the lamp carrying the red glass, push it in and turn to the left. When replacing the lamp portion, engage the bayonet fixing, push in, and turn to the right to secure the body in position.

Stop-lamp Switch. This is operated by the brake rod through a spring. Periodically clean any mud or grease away from the switch, and oil the operating mechanism occasionally with some *thin* oil.

Wiring Connectors. The wiring is connected by means of snap connectors at various convenient places on the motor-cycle, and it is desirable occasionally to check these connectors and see that they are all tight.

Output of Alternator. As there is no voltage regulator or cut-out in the Wipac set, the output is controlled through the lighting switch. A set of two coils from the alternator is directly connected to the rectifier so that, with the lighting switch in the "Off" position and the machine running on coil ignition, the battery is being charged at approximately 0·5 amps when the motor-cycle engine is running at 1,500 r.p.m. This charging rate rises to 2 amps when the "Colt" engine reaches 3,500 r.p.m. and over. When the pilot, rear, and speedometer lamps are switched on the charging rate is approximately 0·5 amps at 1,750 r.p.m., rising to 2 amps at 3,700 r.p.m. and speeds above this. When the headlamp is switched on, this action connects in the second group of coils on the alternator, thus compensating for the extra load. The charging rate in this position is approximately 0·5 amps at 2,000 r.p.m., rising to approximately 2 amps at 3,500 r.p.m. and above.

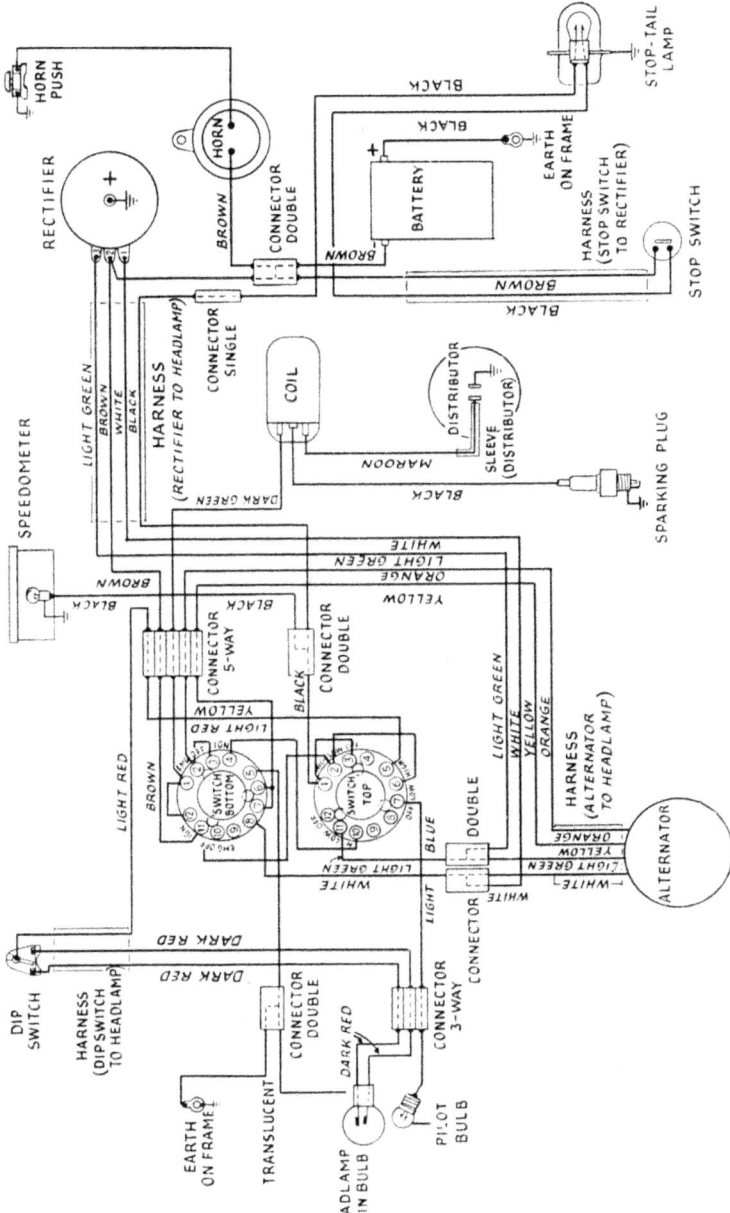

FIG. 26. WIRING DIAGRAM FOR WIPAC LIGHTING EQUIPMENT (1954–5 MODELS)

Applies to 1954–5 Ariel "Colts" with coil ignition, a Series 114 Mark I Wipac alternator, and a stop-tail lamp with a single double-filament bulb. This diagram also applies to 1954–5 "Colts" with a three-bulb stop-tail lamp, except for the connexions to the lamp itself

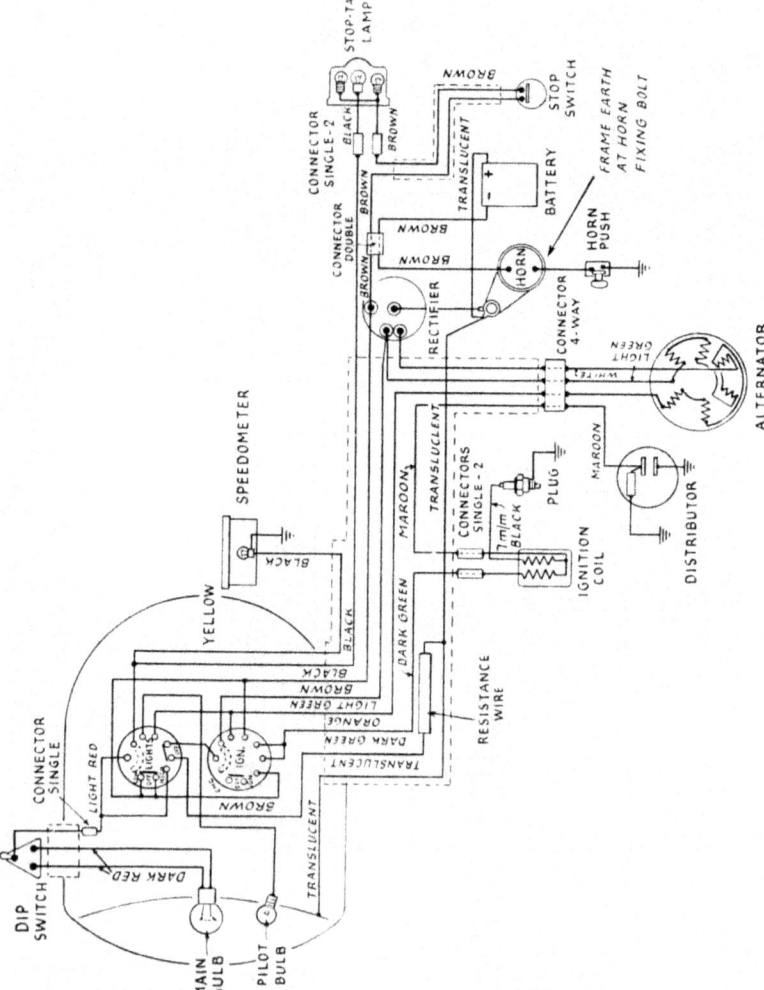

Fig. 27. Wiring Diagram for Wipac Lighting Equipment (1956–60 Models)
Applies to all the later 200 c.c. "Colts" with coil ignition, Wipac alternator, three-bulb stop-tail lamp and separate ignition and lighting switch built into the headlamp

Flat Battery. If the motor-cycle fails to start because of a flat battery, switch over to the "EMG" position. This connects four coils from the alternator directly to the coil, and at the same time it leaves two coils connected to the rectifier; this enables the engine to start; for actual riding switch over immediately to the "IGN" position. The machine will then continue to run satisfactorily as there is sufficient current produced at lowest running speeds to feed the ignition coil and supply the lamps with their needs. *See also* page 49 regarding a disconnected battery.

CHAPTER IV

ARIEL LUBRICATION

Two types of highly efficient dry sump lubrication systems are provided on Ariel S.V. and O.H.V. singles, and the owner-rider is required to provide the minimum amount of maintenance.

Never attempt to economize where lubrication is concerned, otherwise you may cause temporary or permanent damage to the vital metal bearing surfaces and the highly polished cylinder walls and piston surfaces. To

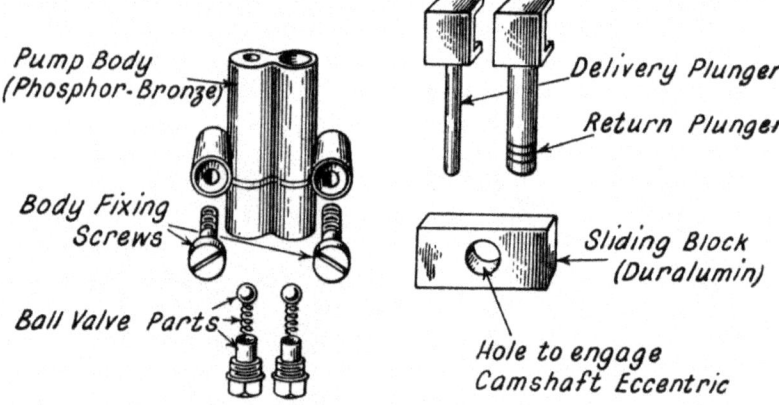

FIG. 28. THE "HEART" OF THE DRY-SUMP LUBRICATION SYSTEM—THE ARIEL CAMSHAFT-DRIVEN DOUBLE-PLUNGER OIL PUMP SHOWN DISMANTLED
Applies to all 1939–59 models except 1954–9 "Colts"

obtain maximum Ariel performance and to keep wear down to the minimum, note and follow the instructions given in this chapter conscientiously. It is particularly important to avoid excessive heat and friction during the running-in period; this enables all bearing surfaces to bed-down correctly and progressively.

ENGINE LUBRICATION

Outline of D.S. Lubrication System No. 1 (1952–60 S.V. and O.H.V. Singles, Except "Colts"). On late 1952 and all subsequent Ariels, except the 1954–9 200 c.c. "Colts," the dry-sump lubrication pump is as shown in Fig. 28. A simple but most effective double-plunger Ariel pump is housed inside the magneto chain-case and is bolted to the outside part of the timing case. Its two vertical plungers move side by side in the bores of the phosphor-bronze body of the pump, shown dismantled in Fig. 28.

As may be seen in Fig. 28, a duralumin sliding block is positioned along the tops of the two plungers, and a hole in the sliding block engages an eccentric on the camshaft. Thus as the camshaft rotates, the delivery and return plungers are caused to move in the bores of the pump body. The pump plungers (*see* Fig. 28) are of two different diameters, but both have the same stroke; consequently the return (bigger) plunger passes more oil than the delivery (smaller) plunger. It sucks oil from the oil tank and passes it through a pipe in the back of the timing cover and projecting into the hollow timing-side mainshaft. The oil is then pressure-fed through an "oil purifier" (in the timing-side flywheel) into the hollow crankpin, and thereby direct to the big-end bearing which gets a continuous flow of clean, cool, engine oil. Emerging from the connecting-rod big-end, the engine oil is projected on to the piston and cylinder bore, effectively keeping their smooth surfaces nicely lubricated and preventing excessive temperatures; afterwards the oil drains down into the crankcase.

The timing case and magneto chain-case are also well lubricated by oil, spray from the crankcase being forced through appropriate vent holes; after attaining a pre-determined level (sufficient to cause the engine timing-pinion to run in an oil-bath) all surplus oil drains back into the crankcase.

At the base of the crankcase, below the timing gear, is a small sump in which the engine oil collects after passing through a large gauze filter. The filtered oil is finally delivered back into the oil tank (which also has a large filter) by means of the oil-pump return plunger (the larger one) and the return pipe for re-circulation. Circulation continues so long as the engine is running, the oil supply to the engine varying according to the engine revolutions. One pint of engine oil is circulated every ten minutes while riding in top gear at 25 m.p.h.

Additional Ball Valves (1957–60 "Magdyno" Models). Besides the two ball valves at the base of the oil pump (*see* Fig. 28) two extra ball valves are provided on all 1957–60 Ariels except the 200 c.c. O.H.V. "Colts."

One additional ball valve is fitted into the timing-case cover in the direct oil-return line. The valve comprises a small coil spring and a $\frac{3}{32}$ in. diameter steel ball; the spring is positioned firstly in an enlarged hole in the aluminium timing-case cover immediately behind the oil pump on the return side, followed by the steel ball. Should you have occasion to remove the oil pump at any time, take great care to see that the steel ball and spring are not accidentally lost, because, although the oil pump will function minus these, there will not be present the additional safeguard against failure in the event of the return oil-pump valve (shown in Fig. 28) becoming inoperative.

The second additional ball valve is fitted in the supply line and ensures against failure of the delivery oil pump caused by the entry of foreign matter in the pump ball valve. The extra valve is located in the feed pipe to the big-end bearing immediately behind the oil pump, and is held in

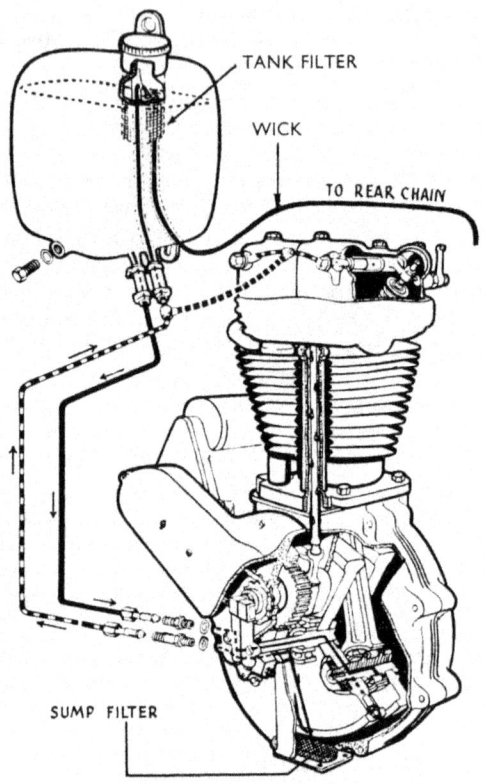

FIG. 29. DIAGRAM SHOWING OIL CIRCULATION ON 1952–60 O.H.V. "MAGDYNO" MODELS

On the S.V. engine (Model VB) there are, of course, no overhead rocker-boxes, and the pipe shown dotted is omitted. On 1941 and all previous Ariel engines an oil regulator is fitted in the timing cover between the oil pump and the main feed into the engine; the oil pipe to the rocker-boxes (O.H.V.) is taken from near the oil pump to the exhaust rocker spindle (instead of midway between the inlet and exhaust rocker spindles); the wick to the secondary chain is also omitted. On 1939–41 models an oil pressure gauge (on the petrol tank) is included, and its pipe leads to the oil pressure regulator. On all earlier models the oil-tank filter is close to the orifice for the delivery oil pipe

position by a small plug. It also comprises a coil spring and a $\frac{3}{16}$ in. diameter steel ball, the spring being inserted first into the feed pipe, followed by the ball and plug.

Outline of D.S. Lubricating System No. 2 (1954–60 200 c.c. O.H.V. "Colts"). Like the remaining O.H.V. singles, the lightweight "Colts" have a dry sump system. The "heart" of the system, however, instead of comprising a double-plunger pump, consists of a double-gear oil pump positioned at the bottom of the crankcase. All oilways are internal with

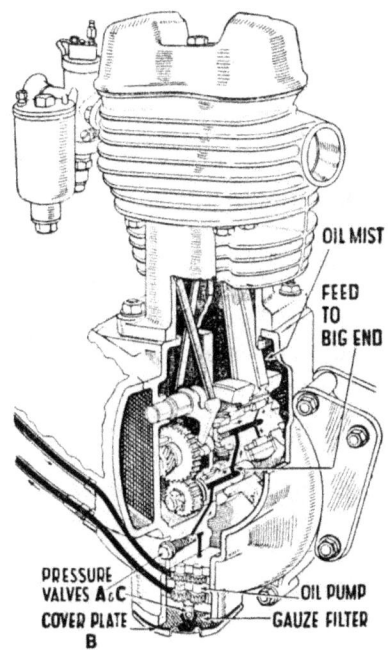

Fig. 30. Diagram Showing Oil Circulation on 1954–60 O.H.V. Coil-ignition Models

Applicable to all 200 c.c. "Colt" models. Two types of oil tanks (*see* Figs. 34–35) are provided, and 1956–60 engines have an external oil feed to the rocker-box (*see* Fig. 35)

the exception of the delivery and return oil pipes from the oil tank, and (on 1956–9 models) the oil pipe to the rocker-box. The engine oil flows from the oil tank through a large filter (*see* Figs. 34 and 35) in the tank, to the feed part of the oil pump; this forces it past a pressure valve (*A*) (*see* Fig. 30) to the drilled crankshaft and the connecting-rod big-end bearing.

Having thoroughly lubricated the roller bearing of the connecting-rod and circulated throughout the engine as oil mist, the engine oil drains through a gauze filter at the base of the crankcase. Afterwards it is sucked by the return part of the gear pump past another ball valve (*C*), and is pressure-fed back into the oil tank through the oil-return pipe. Circulation continues in this manner so long as the engine continues to rotate.

On 1956–60 "Colt" engines an auxiliary oil pipe (*see* Fig. 35) supplies engine oil direct to the rocker-box on the cylinder head.

Five Points to Remember. Whatever Ariel model you have, there are five essential points to observe. They are—
1. A new engine must be run-in with great care.
2. Sufficient oil must be kept in circulation.
3. The oil must be of good quality.
4. The oil must be kept clean.
5. Oil dilution must not occur.

Suitable Engine Oils (1939–60 "Magdyno" Models). To obtain maximum performance from your Ariel engine, with the least amount of wear, Ariel Motors, Ltd. recommend the use of one of the following high-grade engine oils (not tabulated in any special order)—
1. Castrol Grand Prix (XXL during winter).
2. Mobiloil D (BB during winter).
3. Shell X 100–40 (X 100–30 during winter).
4. B.P. Energol SAE 40 (SAE 30 during winter).
5. Essolube 50 (40 during winter).

Suitable Engine Oils (1954–60 200 c.c. "Colts"). For the coil-ignition lightweight models Ariel Motors, Ltd. recommend the use of one of the following oils—
1. Castrol Grand Prix (XL during winter).
2. Mobiloil D (A during winter).
3. Shell X 100–50 (30 during winter).
4. B.P. Energol SAE 50 (SAE 30 during winter).
5. Essolube 50 (30 during winter).

Running-in. General advice on running-in the engine during the first 1,000–1,500 miles is given on page 16, and the author would again emphasize the importance of these instructions. With regard to lubrication during the running-in period, the makers recommend the use of some upper-cylinder lubricant (*see* page 17), and it is important to keep the level of oil in the tank high and to change the oil regularly.

Changing the Oil During Running-in. During the running-in period it is advisable to change the whole of the oil in the oil tank at about 200, 500, and 1,000 miles. This effects the immediate removal of any metallic particles and foreign matter which may get into circulation during this period.

Maintain the Correct Oil Level. It is desirable to inspect the level of the oil in the oil tank about every 250 miles, and to top up with the correct brand and grade of oil if necessary. Every time the oil is changed it is advisable to remove and clean both oil filters. On the singles do not fill the oil tank above 1 in. below the return pipe and do not let the level drop below about two-thirds. On most 1939–58 models there is a mark on the outside of the oil tank, and it is important never to allow the oil inside the tank to fall below this level.

Checking Oil Circulation. On all Ariels the double-plunger, or gear-type ("Colts"), oil pump pressure-feeds the engine automatically with engine oil, and a regular flow of lubricant is fed back into the oil tank via the return pipe. To check the oil circulation it is therefore only necessary to remove the oil-tank filler cap (*see* Fig. 31) and observe the oil flowing from the oil-return pipe orifice. It is advisable to check the oil circulation fairly frequently, as the procedure is so extremely simple.

For a few seconds after starting up, the oil returns in a continuous stream, but the flow gradually diminishes as all surplus oil in the engine is returned to the tank by the larger capacity pump-plunger or gear train ("Colts"). Note that an oil flow in the form of a series of bubbles is quite normal and must not be regarded as an insufficient return of engine oil.

The Pressure Gauge (1939–41 Models). An oil pressure gauge is mounted on the petrol tank on 1939–41 Ariels, and the engine has an oil-pressure regulator for adjusting the oil pressure recorded on the gauge. Fig. 31 shows a diagram of the complete lubrication system.

Keep an eye on the position of the oil pressure gauge needle, but note that so long as an oil pressure is recorded, this indicates that the oil is circulating normally. Should the oil pressure gauge needle remain near zero, immediately check the oil flow in the oil tank as previously described.

When starting up the engine from *cold* the oil pressure may vary considerably from the normal reading, but as the oil warms up the oil pressure reading should not exceed 15 lb per sq in., or fall below 10 lb per sq in.

Note that if the valve clearances (on an O.H.V. engine) are excessive, oil leakage at the joints between the push-rods and overhead rockers occurs, and this tends to reduce the oil pressure. Therefore maintain the valve clearances correct. Note that when an engine is just ticking-over the oil pressure reading may fall to only about 5 lb per sq in., but it should rise to 10–15 lb per sq in. when the motor-cycle is actually ridden.

The Oil Pressure Regulator (1939–41). To enable the oil pressure gauge to be set to give the normal reading of 10–15 lb per sq in., an oil pressure regulator is incorporated between the oil pump and the oil feed to the engine. Details are shown in Fig. 32. The regulator body is screwed into the right-hand side of the pump housing below the pump, and contains at its inner end a ball valve operated by a coil compression spring partly enclosed in a brass ferrule able to slide in the regulator body. At the other end is an external adjuster screw with lock-nut. By screwing up or unscrewing the adjuster screw the pressure required to lift the ball off its seat

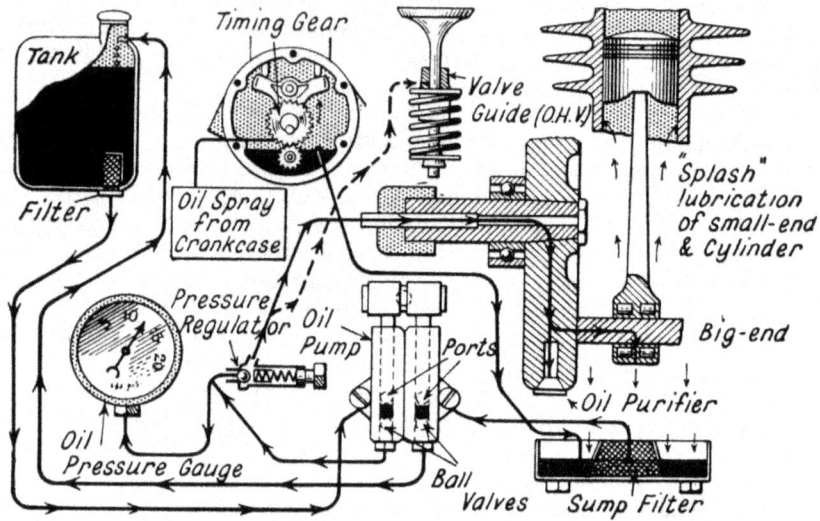

FIG. 31. DIAGRAM SHOWING THE 1939–41 DRY-SUMP LUBRICATION SYSTEM
Note the arrangement of the oil pressure gauge and the oil pressure regulator

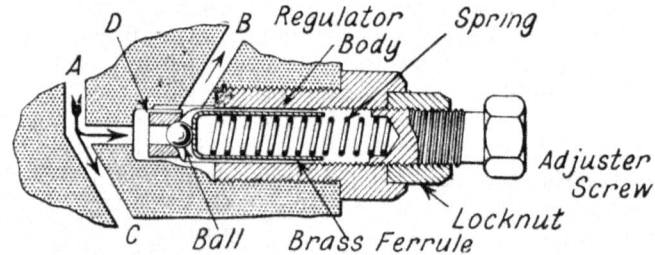

FIG. 32. THE OIL PRESSURE REGULATOR (1939–41 SINGLES)

can be varied. Oil from the pump passing along the passage (*A*) cannot enter the passage (*B*) leading to the engine until it has first lifted the ball off its seat; and since the oil in the passage (*A*) is in direct communication with the oil pressure gauge via the passage (*C*), the pressure registered by the oil gauge is equal to the pressure needed to pass the ball valve. To enable the gauge needle to return to zero when the engine stops, the inner end of the regulator body is made slightly smaller than the hole into which it fits, so that oil leaks back from the gauge between them at the point (*D*). Once the pressure regulator has been adjusted to give the correct gauge reading it should not subsequently be interfered with. On all O.H.V. engines with an external oil feed to the rocker spindles and valve guides, the hexagon-headed adjuster screw is situated immediately above the junction of the oil feed pipe and the timing case. On all models, the oil pressure is *increased* or decreased by turning the screw *clockwise* or anti-clockwise respectively.

On the single-cylinder models increasing the oil pressure has no effect whatever, and the regulator is only provided to enable a normal reading of 10–15 lb per sq in. to be obtained. The quantity of oil passed into the engine is governed solely by the efficiency of the pump and the speed of the engine.

Checking Oil Circulation (1939–41). Remove the plug above the oil pressure regulator, when, with engine ticking over, oil will be pumped out at this point instead of passing along the oil-ways to the mainshaft and big-end bearings.

The 1942 and later engines have no oil pressure regulator, and the oil supply from the pump can be tested by detaching the lower end of the oil-pipe to the rocker-box, and noting whether oil flows from the union stud when the engine is running.

Oil Pressure Fluctuation (1939–41). This should immediately divert the rider's attention to the oil level in the tank. If the level is found to be correct (*see* page 59) obviously a shortage of oil is not causing the trouble, and the most likely alternative is that some dirt in the pressure regulator is causing the ball valve to misbehave. In this case the regulator (Fig. 32) should be dismantled and cleaned. When refitting, see that the closed end of the brass ferrule is next to the ball. The order of reassembly is: ball valve, ferrule, spring, adjuster screw, and lock-nut.

The Ariel dry-sump lubrication system rarely gives trouble, and when trouble does arise it is generally due to the use of dirty oil. The remedy is to remove and clean (*a*) the oil pressure regulator, (*b*) both filters, (*c*) the oil purifier. If the engine oil in the tank has been in use for a considerable time, drain completely and replenish with clean oil. In the case of the single-cylinder models it is necessary to remove the magneto chain-case cover in order to gain access to the pump valves.

Oil Pressure Valve (1942 Onwards). Since 1941 the oil pressure regulator has been replaced by a spring-loaded ball valve located in the oil feed pipe to the engine mainshaft on all "Magdyno" models.

After a big mileage the spring may weaken and require to be renewed. To remove the ball valve, first detach the "Magdyno" chain-case cover and the oil pump. You will notice just behind the pump a small hole (drilled in the timing case cover). A shouldered steel plug fits into this hole, and on S.V. engines is slotted. Remove the plug (a press fit) by turning it slightly and then withdrawing it, using the pointed jaws of a small pair of pliers. Then remove the spring and steel ball from the big-end feed pipe. On assembly fit in this order: the spring; steel ball; the plug. Tap the plug home.

Sources of Heavy Oil Consumption (All "Magdyno" Models). Possible sources of a marked rise in consumption are given below.

(*a*) Wear of the cylinder barrel, piston, or piston rings; or perhaps scoring or metal pick-up due to a partial or complete seizure. The remedy is to renew worn parts or have a rebore and a new oversize piston fitted.

(*b*) A dirty condition of the whole circulation system which allows foreign matter to reach the valve situated below the scavenge plunger of the oil pump. Judging by the oil return to the tank, the oil pump may appear to be functioning perfectly, but some foreign matter adhering to the above-mentioned valve may cause inefficient scavenging, with the result that oil is not properly cleared from the engine sump. In consequence the flywheels dip into the oil and cause high consumption due to excessive splash. The remedy is to clean the whole system out and replenish with clean oil (*see* notes on pressure fluctuation given on page 59). Special attention should be paid to the cleanliness of the pump valves and the pump itself. It is advisable to renew both the springs (*see* Fig. 28).

(*c*) Air leakage between the oil pump and the engine sump. Leakage may occur at one or more points. For instance, the sump pipe may be slack in the crankcase. Verify whether it is firm. Again, the body of the oil pump may be a poor fit on the timing-cover face. Check whether a paper washer is fitted and verify that the washer holes do register with the pump ports. Check the pump securing screws for tightness. In some circumstances the fitting of an extra paper washer is beneficial. The author vividly remembers a D.R. bringing an Ariel into Chiswick Police Station when the author was in the M.P.W.R. It just would not run, but when the author fitted a new washer the right way round, all trouble vanished!

(*d*) An air leak between the crankcase boss and the back of the timing cover. Such leakage sometimes occurs at the point where the oil return pipe projects from the boss inside the timing case. An additional paper washer (0·005 in. thick) should be fitted at this point. The timing cover, after a big mileage has been covered, sometimes takes a "set" away from the crankcase with the result that air leakage persists even after an extra washer has been fitted. The remedy is to fit a third washer, but avoid fitting too many washers, otherwise the timing cover may be strained.

(*e*) A partial stoppage in the oil return system. If this occurs, take off the pipe leading from the oil tank to the timing cover and blow through it. Test the oil-ways in the timing cover by removing the oil pump and squirting paraffin down each duct with an oil-gun. Place its nozzle against the appropriate port in the timing cover face and check that there is no obstruction in the oil-way running from the face of the timing cover down through the sump pipe. To ascertain whether paraffin emerges freely from the sump pipe, it is necessary to detach the sump base.

(*f*) Wear of the double-plunger oil pump. Wear may develop after a very big mileage, and oil circulation may be appreciably affected as well as consumption. If this happens, fit a new pump or return the old one to the Service Dept. of Ariel Motors, Ltd. for attention, if this is practicable.

(*g*) Oil loss through the breather pipe. Engine oil may be ejected through the breather pipe situated beneath the "Magdyno" chain-case. This is generally caused by an incomplete oil return to the tank, but it may also be due to the fact that the connecting union is not screwed home far enough. Screw it up as far as possible, and check that the non-return ball valve is in place. The valve comprises a $\frac{1}{4}$ in. steel ball inserted into the outer end of the union and a split brass ring retained by the end of the breather-pipe nipple.

Seating of Ball Valves (1954–60 "Colts"). Referring to Fig. 30, note that incorrect seating of the ball valve (*A*) will permit engine oil to flow from the oil tank into the engine when the latter is not running. Should such leakage occur, unscrew the plug over the valve and remove both the spring and the ball. Clean the ball and its seating, and replace the parts.

In the event of the ball valve (*C*) in the base of the pump adhering to its seating, no oil will be pressure-fed back into the oil tank. To remedy this annoying trouble (somewhat rare), first remove the cover plate (*B*); then insert a piece of stiff wire into the valve orifice and lift the ball off its seating to free it. When replacing the cover plate (*B*) be careful not to overtighten its securing nuts; tighten the four nuts evenly with a *small* spanner. If not perfect, renew the cover-plate washers. Also make sure that the gauze filter is absolutely clean.

Removing Oil Purifier Plug ("Magdyno" Models). Referring to Fig. 33, the dirt and impurities which have collected in the cupped plug (*D*) must be cleared away at least every 5,000–8,000 miles under normal conditions of use. Where an Ariel is ridden in particularly dusty conditions, causing a proportionately greater amount of dust to be sucked in through the air-intake of the Amal carburettor, it is advisable to remove the plug for cleaning at substantially shorter intervals. Indeed it is good general practice to remove the plug each time the oil tank and sump filters are being attended to.

To attend to the oil purifier, first undo the four set-bolts and drop the sump, complete with filter. Rotate the engine until the cupped plug (*D*) is immediately *above* the sump and then unscrew the plug; it is locked by being bell-mouthed. When the plug is removed, the dirt and impurities (if present in any quantity) will be found packed quite hard inside the cup formed in the plug, and must be removed with the blade of a penknife. See that the tube (A) is not damaged, and if it drops out, replace with the large end in the plug. The plug locates the tube and retains it in position. The tube (A) is omitted on 1939-45 "Red Hunter" Ariels, and on *all* 1946-60 models.

When replacing the plug, see that it is screwed up dead tight. On all engines the plug of the oil purifier is, as previously mentioned, locked in position by being slightly bell-mouthed so that it binds in the thread. No

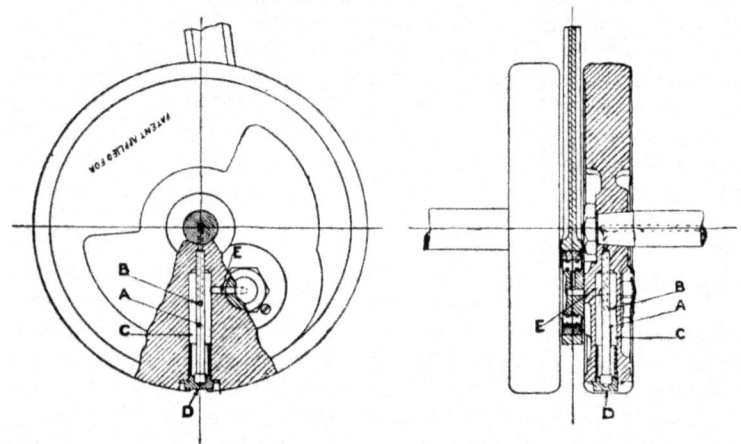

FIG. 33. DETAILS OF THE OIL PURIFIER
This acts on the centrifugal principle and is provided on all 1939-60 "Magdyno" models

further locking is provided or necessary so long as the plug binds slightly and is screwed firmly home. It should be noted that when the cylinder barrel is removed during decarbonizing it is more convenient to remove the plug from the *top* rather than from the bottom.

Change Engine Oil and Clean Tank Filters Regularly. On the "Magdyno" models and the coil-ignition models ("Colts") it is recommended that the engine oil in the tank be changed, and the filter cleaned, about every 1,500 miles and 2,000 miles respectively.

Although the Ariel oil purifier will remove all dirt and impurities, it cannot convert old oil into new, and it therefore becomes necessary to throw away the used and contaminated oil, which loses its good lubricating properties. During the running-in period (*see* page 17) more frequent changing of the engine oil is desirable. Always drain out the old oil (preferably after a run) when the engine oil is *still warm*, wash out the oil tank with flushing oil, clean the filter thoroughly in petrol, dry it, and replenish the tank with new engine oil of the correct type (*see* page 58).

The Oil Tank Filter. On earlier "Magdyno" models (pre-1952) unscrew the hexagon plug at the base of the tank; see that the oil supply pipe, which projects right into the tank in line with the filter, is located inside the gauze on assembly, and screw up the hexagon plug securely.

On all later (1952 onwards) "Magdyno" models the tank filter provided is of the type shown in Fig. 29. To remove the large filter, unscrew the

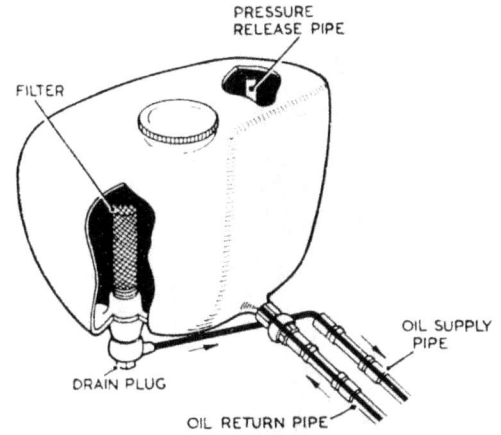

FIG. 34. THE OIL TANK, FILTER, AND PIPES FITTED TO 1954-5 ARIEL "COLTS"

1956-60 200 c.c O.H.V. models include an oil pipe to the rocker-box (*see* Fig. 35)

filler cap and carefully lift the filter out; cleaning can then be proceeded with.

On the 1954-5 200 c.c. coil-ignition Ariel "Colts" (Model LH) a cylindrical type of gauze filter is fitted as shown in Fig. 34. To remove the filter for thorough cleaning, unscrew the oil supply pipe union at the bottom of the oil tank and the filter will come away with the plug.

On 1956-60 "Colts" the type of oil tank and large filter provided is shown in Fig. 35. To remove this filter, unscrew the filler cap and withdraw the filter from the tank.

The Sump Filter. On all Ariels this is located at the bottom of the crankcase immediately below the double-plunger or gear-type oil pump (*see* Figs. 29 and 30 respectively). You are advised to remove and thoroughly clean the sump filter in petrol each time the engine oil is changed and the oil-tank filter is cleaned (*see* page 64).

On all "Magdyno" models to remove the sump filter after flushing out the oil tank and kicking the engine over, unscrew the four set-bolts and withdraw the combined cover-plate and gauze filter. During replacement see that the suction pipe is located in the hole in the top of the gauze, and check that the joint washer is in sound condition. Finally wire up the four set-bolts.

On all 200 c.c. coil-ignition "Colts," to remove the flat gauze-filter it is only necessary to remove the steel cover-plate ((*B*) in Fig. 30) after removing the four securing-nuts. When replacing, check that the joint

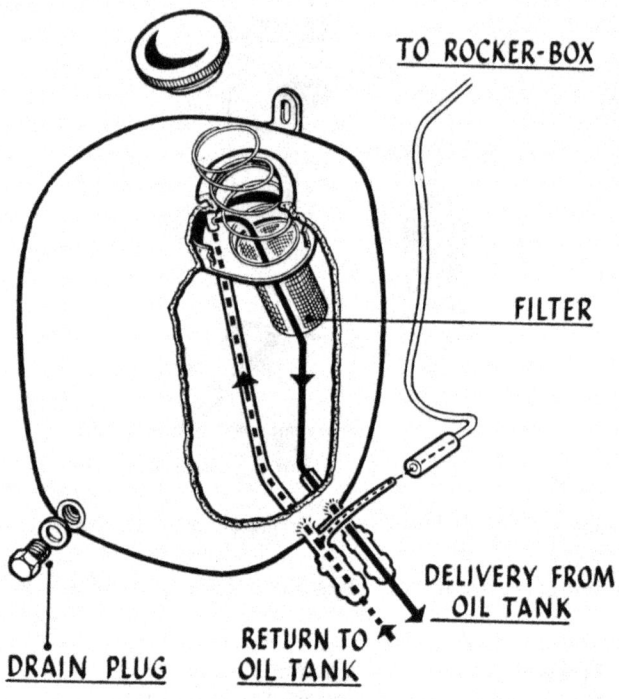

Fig. 35. The Oil Tank, Filter, and Pipe Provided on 1956–60 Ariel "Colts"

This diagram shows the oil pipe to the rocker-box

washers are perfect and be very careful to tighten the four nuts with an appropriate spanner, doing this uniformly and without excessive pressure, to avoid damaging the studs.

The Supply and Return Oil Pipes. Should it become necessary for any reason to remove the two main oil pipes, make absolutely sure that the pipes are correctly assembled. The oil *supply* pipe from the oil tank must be connected to the *top* screwed union on the crankcase. The oil *return* pipe must be connected to the *lower* screwed union on the crankcase.

ARIEL LUBRICATION

Rocker-box Lubrication. On all 1939–60 Ariel engines automatic lubrication for the rocker-boxes or rocker-box ("Colts") is provided, the oil supply in practically all instances (except 1954–5 "Colts") being provided by an auxiliary oil pipe leading from the oil return pipe from the crankcase to the oil tank, close to the tank itself (*see* Fig. 29). No manual attention is necessary other than to see that all connexions are kept clean

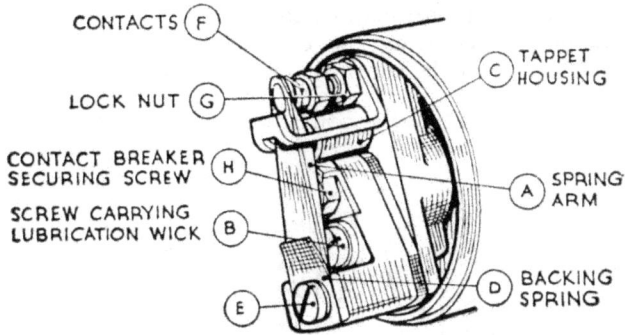

Fig. 36. Face Cam Contact-breaker of Lucas "Magdyno" Shown Assembled

This type of contact-breaker is provided on the magnetos of all 1939–60 "Magdynos." The various parts are shown dismantled in Fig. 37

and tight. On 1939–41 models with an oil pressure gauge and regulator the oil feed pipe is taken from the crankcase at a point close to the oil pressure regulator (*see* Fig. 31).

Bearings of Lucas "Magdynos." These are initially packed with grease by the makers during assembly and further greasing should not be necessary for about two years. When a general overhaul becomes necessary it is desirable to remove the "Magdyno" and return it to Joseph Lucas, Ltd. of Birmingham, 19, or to one of their service depots, for thorough servicing.

No grease nipples are fitted, but the contact-breaker requires periodical oiling by the Ariel rider. About every 2,500 miles insert a few drops of thin machine oil into the lubricator on the commutator end-bracket of an E3HM dynamo (*see* Fig. 13). The driving-side bearing is packed with grease and on a new machine should last until it is stripped down for a general overhaul.

The "Magdyno" Contact-breaker. The cam and tappet of the face-cam type contact-breaker (Fig. 36) require lubrication approximately every 3,000 miles. In order to effect such lubrication, remove the complete contact-breaker as described below.

First release the spring blade and take off the contact-breaker cover.

Now, referring to Figs. 36 and 37, remove the screw (*E*) and the spring washer retaining the spring arm (*A*) to the body (*L*) of the contact-breaker, and detach the curved backing-spring (*D*) and the spring arm (*A*). Next unscrew the screw (*B*) carrying the lubrication wick, and remove the insulating bush (fibre). Straighten the tab on the locking plate (*J*) situated behind the head of the contact-breaker securing screw (*H*), and with the magneto spanner remove screw (*H*). Then lever off the contact-breaker body (*L*) from the armature-shaft extension.

After completely removing the contact-breaker, saturate the wick, mounted in the core of the carrying screw (*B*), with a few drops of *thin*

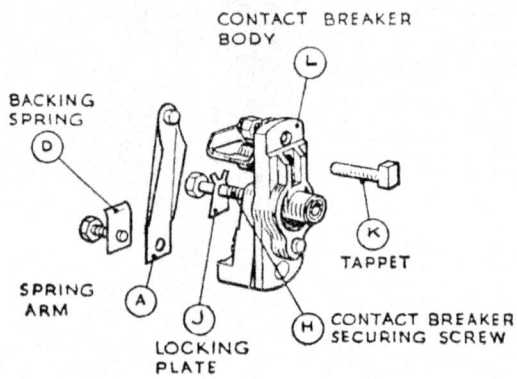

Fig. 37. Face Cam Contact-breaker of Lucas "Magdyno" Shown Dismantled

The same contact-breaker is shown assembled in Fig. 36
(*By courtesy of Associated Motor Cycles, Ltd.*)

machine oil. Push from the contact-breaker body (*L*) the tappet (*K*) and wipe the tappet clean with a soft cloth. Smear a little thin machine oil on the tappet and replace it in the body.

To assemble the face-cam type contact-breaker, proceed in the reverse order of dismantling. Make sure that the curved backing spring (*D*) is replaced so that the curved part is on the *outside*.

The Wipac Contact-breaker (1954–60 "Colts"). On the 200 c.c. Ariel "Colts" the Wipac contact-breaker unit is positioned on the off-side of the engine, and is immediately accessible on removing the large circular coverplate secured by two screws (*see* Fig. 45). The contact-breaker unit has a felt pad for lubricating the cam, and this pad should be fed with a few drops of engine oil about every 1,000 miles. Be careful not to oil the pad excessively, otherwise some oil may reach the contacts of the contact-breaker and cause considerable trouble.

LUBRICATING MOTOR-CYCLE PARTS

Lubricating the Burman Gearbox. Ariel Motors, Ltd. advise the use of *summer-grade engine oil* (see page 58) for the four-speed heavyweight Burman gearbox on the 1952–60 models. Exceptions: use Castrol XXL and Mobiloil BB. On 1939–51 machines, however, *light grease* is recommended for gearbox lubrication. On no account must *thick* grease be used. Suitable brands of grease for 1939–51 gearboxes are as follows—

1. Castrolease Medium.
2. Mobilgrease No. 2.
3. Shell Retinax Grease C.D.
4. B.P. Energrease C3.
5. Esso (pressure gun) Grease.

Do not completely fill up the gearbox with engine oil or light grease. Under normal conditions it is sufficient to top up the lubricant every 1,000 miles with 2 fluid oz of light grease or engine oil (1952–60 models) via the grease nipple on the kick-starter case or through the filler-cap orifice on the top edge of the kick-starter end casing. Excessive filling causes leaks.

All 1952 and later Burman gearboxes have an oil-level plug located also on the kick-starter end casing; to top up the gearbox to the maximum permissible level, it is only necessary to pour in engine oil through the filler-cap orifice until it begins to trickle from the level-plug hole. Where a lubricator is provided, grease the pivot for the foot gear-change pedal every 500 miles.

On the earlier four-speed gearboxes, when topping up, also grease the enclosed foot-change mechanism, the kick-starter lever bearing, and the spiral gears for the speedometer drive via the grease nipples provided. The grease nipple for the enclosed foot-change mechanism will be found on the top of the housing cover.

Changing Gearbox Lubricant. After the first 500 miles and thereafter about every 3,000 miles (2,000 miles on "Colts") change the lubricant in the gearbox. The light grease or engine oil (1952–60 models) should be drained completely, the Burman gearbox flushed out with a suitable flushing oil and afterwards replenished with 1 lb 14 oz of light grease (1939–51 boxes), or with 1 pint of engine oil (1952 onwards). The capacity on a 200 c.c. "Colt" is ½ pint.

The screwed drain plug is located low down at the rear of the gearbox shell. Where a non-fluid lubricant (light grease) is used, it may be found somewhat difficult to drain the gearbox thoroughly by removing the drain plug only. The best plan here is to remove the foot-change cover and also the kick-starter case. Before replenishing the gearbox make sure that the drain plug is replaced and firmly tightened.

Clutch Lubrication. Every 250–500 miles the external clutch-lever pivot (pre-1952) should be oiled; every 2,500 miles the clutch operating rod should be removed from the hollow mainshaft and greased. It is particularly important that this long rod should be able to slide backwards and forwards with absolute freedom, otherwise it is impossible to maintain an "easy" clutch action.

Do not forget to keep the external actuating lever (pre-1952) well lubricated, particularly at the point where it is in contact with the plunger.

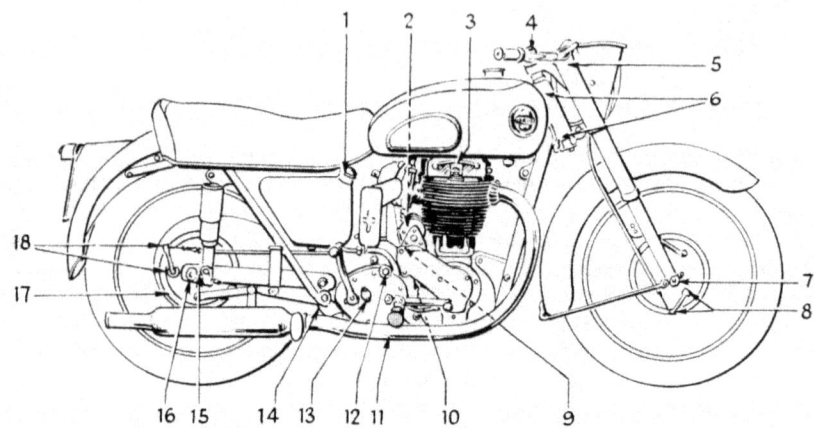

Fig. 38. Showing General Location of Important Lubrication Points on Typical "Magdyno" Model

The bracketed numbers indicate the pages in this chapter where the corresponding full lubrication instructions are given. The sump filter and some of the lesser lubrication points are not indicated

1. Oil tank, filter (page 59)
2. Dynamo, magneto (page 67)
3. Rocker-boxes (page 67)
4. Handlebar controls (page 74)
5. Front forks (page 74)
6. Steering head (page 73)
7. Front hub (page 73)
8. Front brake (page 74)
9. Contact-breaker (page 67)
10. Primary chain (page 70)
11. Central stand (page 76)
12. Gearbox (page 69)
13. Clutch (page 70)
14. Rear-brake pedal (page 70)
15. Speedometer gearbox (page 74)
16. Rear hub (page 73)
17. Secondary chain (page 71)
18. Rear brake (page 74)

During a general overhaul the roller bearing of the clutch sprocket should be removed and packed with grease.

The Engine Shaft Shock Absorber. On all machines with an oil-bath chain-case the shock absorber is automatically lubricated by the oil in the chain-case.

The Primary Chain. The primary chain runs at a high speed, and it is therefore important to keep it well lubricated. On oil-bath chain-case models the chain lower-run dips into the oil, and provided the oil level is maintained correct, the chain will continue to be properly lubricated. The oil bath itself should be replenished with engine oil whenever necessary. Top up the level through the filler orifice to the "oil level plug," (Fig. 39) but do not put excessive oil in or it will possibly be thrown out of the oil-bath chain-case where the mainshaft of the gearbox enters; clutch slip

FIG. 39. OIL-BATH CHAIN-CASE "MAGDYNO" MODELS (PRE-1953)
A smart aluminium oil-bath chain-case with quickly-detachable clutch cover is fitted to all 1953–8 Ariels, except the 1954–9 200 c.c. "Colt" which has a slotted filler cap and screwed oil-level plug
1. Filler cap   2. Oil level plug

may also occur. Always top up with the motor-cycle on *level* ground. Check the level every 500 miles (every 1,000 miles on 200 c.c. "Colts").

About every 2,000 miles flush out the oil-bath chain-case thoroughly and top up with fresh engine oil (*see* page 58) to the correct level. Always be sure that the oil-level plug is *firmly* tightened.

The Secondary Chain. On 1939–55 "Magdyno" models with an oil-bath primary-chain case automatic lubrication of the secondary chain is effected by an overflow from the oil-bath primary-chain case. This overflow functions only when the engine is running, and can be controlled by means of a needle valve located just behind the clutch dome. Observe the general condition of the secondary chain while riding, and if it seems at all dry increase the lubricant overflow by turning the needle-valve adjuster head *anti-clockwise*. Every 500 miles inspect the chain for correct lubrication. On the 1954–8 "Colts" no automatic lubrication of the secondary chain is provided. In this case, and whenever any chain seems to be running dry, apply some engine oil to the chain lower-run while turning over the rear wheel; alternatively with a fairly stiff brush, smear some good grease on the chain.

From time to time (say about once every 2,000 miles) it is a good plan to remove the secondary chain and immerse it in a bath of paraffin. The chain should be allowed to soak well to ensure all the dirt from the rollers being removed, and afterwards be hung up to dry. When the chain has been cleaned it is wise to lubricate it before refitting it to the sprockets.

Immerse the chain for at least *ten minutes* in a suitable receptacle containing Mobilgrease No. 2, B.P. Energol A.O., Esso Fluid Grease, or

FIG. 40. SHOWING DETAILS OF (LEFT) AUTOMATIC OILING AND (RIGHT) COMPLETE ENCLOSURE OF SECONDARY CHAIN ON 1956–60 "MAGDYNO" MODELS

The automatic lubrication is specified whether or not complete enclosure of the chain is specified. It does not, however, apply to any 200 c.c. Ariel "Colts"

(*By courtesy of "Motor Cycle," London*)

Castrolease Grease Graphited. The grease should be heated until just fluid, and maintained in this state during the period of chain immersion.

Having lubricated the chain, fit it to the gearbox and rear wheel sprockets. It is permissible to lubricate the chain, using engine oil instead of one of the greases mentioned but this substitute is not so good. Allow the chain to soak for a considerable period when engine oil is used.

On 1956–60 "Magdyno" models complete enclosure of the chain is, or can be, provided, together with automatic lubrication of the chain by means of an ingenious total-loss system. This takes the form of an orifice and collector pad, positioned in the mouth of the oil tank opposite the oil return pipe orifice. Some lubricant is splashed on the collector pad and filtered through it; it passes through a special feed pipe leading from the base of the oil tank to a grummet in the shroud which encases the gearbox sprocket for the secondary chain. The feed is continued by a flexible pipe and oil is conveyed, at the rate of one drop every three or four minutes, to the secondary chain behind the sprocket just mentioned.

Suitable Greases. Grease nipples are provided for motor-cycle parts which need regular greasing, and a Tecalemit grease-gun for grease injection is recommended. Certain parts require to be lubricated with engine oil (*see* page 58) and oil caps or oil holes with protective spring covers are fitted for this purpose. Always use a high quality grease. Suitable greases, recommended by Ariel Motors, Ltd. for general greasing, are as follows—

1. Lithium Base Grease.
2. Shell Retinax CD.
3. Castrolease CL.
4. Esso Grease.
5. B.P. Energrease C3.

Grease containers designed for quick filling of the grease-gun are available and obviate the messy job of filling the gun by hand.

The Steering Head. Two grease nipples are provided for the ball bearings in the steering head, and the grease-gun should be applied to them about once every 1,000 miles.

Greasing Wheel Bearings. It is most important to keep the bearings of both hubs thoroughly greased, as they are called upon to carry heavy stresses. Be careful not to apply excessive grease because this can result in grease being forced into the brake drums, thereby resulting in the brakes losing considerable efficiency. Where a sidecar outfit is concerned, do not omit to lubricate the hub of the sidecar wheel.

Suitable greases for lubricating the hubs of "Magdyno" Ariels are: B.P. Energrease C3, Shell Retinax RB, Lithium Base Grease, Castrolease Heavy, and Esso Grease. Suitable greases for lubricating the hubs of 1954–60 200 c.c. Ariel "Colts" are: B.P. Energrease C3, Shell Retinax A or RB, Lithium Base Grease, Wakefield Castrolease Heavy, and Esso Grease.

On the 200 c.c. "Colts" about every 1,000 miles inject *grease* (three to four strokes) through the nipple in the centre of each hub. Where lubricators are provided, similarly lubricate the hubs on all "Magdyno" models. Where lubricators are not provided, every 3,000 miles remove both hubs, clean, and carefully repack the hubs by hand with grease.

On "Magdyno" models (with full-width hubs) from 1956 onwards every 3,000 miles remove the front-hub spindle, insert a small quantity of grease, and replace the hub spindle. On 1956 and later "Magdyno" models every 3,000 miles insert a small quantity of grease by hand through the right-hand side of the rear-hub tube.

The Front and Rear Brakes. Grease the front and rear brake-cam spindles every 500 miles (every 1,000 miles on "Colts"). Also grease the rear-brake pedal pivot and all other points where lubricators are fitted. On the "Colt" a few drops of engine oil are needed, not grease, for the brake-pedal pivot. Apply the oil can regularly to all exposed cable ends, joints, and exposed linkage. Do not forget the handlebar lever.

Saddle Nose-bolt (O.H.V. "Colts"). Grease occasionally with grease-gun.

Sidecar Chassis. To prevent a tendency to squeak it is wise to grease occasionally with graphite the front and rear ball-jointed connexions. Also grease periodically the sliding joint at the base of the seat pillar connexion tube.

Control Levers. It is possible to postpone the time when cable breakages occur by occasionally oiling or greasing the cables at places where they are apt to bind on the control mechanism on the handlebars. It is advisable when fitting new cables to charge the casings with grease.

The Speedometer Gearbox. On "Magdyno" and "Colt" models every 1,000 miles apply the grease-gun to the nipple on the speedometer gearbox (where provided).

Plunger-type Rear Suspension (1939–54). To obtain maximum benefit from the efficient rear-springing system, always attend to grease lubrication regularly. No other attention is required. Referring to Fig. 82, apply the grease-gun about every 250–300 miles to the nipple on the head of each clamp bolt and also to the nipple on the pivot-pin boss.

"Swinging Arm" Rear Suspension. Both of the rear-suspension units are sealed and do not require to be topped up. The "swinging arm" pivot requires no lubrication, and its mounting bushes will give very long service.

Plunger-type Rear Suspension (1954–60). On 200 c.c. O.H.V. "Colts" apply the grease-gun weekly to the grease nipple (4, Fig. 73) on each suspension unit. Also occasionally smear the chromium-plated area where movement occurs with a little oil or grease. This will minimize any tendency to corrode.

Dipping Switch. Lubricate the moving parts of the dipping switch about every 5,000 miles, using a *little* thin machine oil.

The Telescopic Front Forks. These are designed for long use without attention, and topping up of the oil is normally unnecessary. At long intervals (10,000 miles at least), however, if the forks appear to have lost effective hydraulic damping, and develop excessive up-and-down movement, drain each fork leg and fill (1956-8 models) with *one-third* of a pint ("Magdyno" models) or *one-quarter* of a pint ("Colts") of new oil of the correct type as described in the following paragraphs.

Draining and Refilling Front Forks (1956–60 "Magdyno" Models.) First remove the screw-type plug from the top of each fork leg (*A*, Fig. 21). Next remove the drain plug at the bottom of each fork tube and drain off the oil into a suitable receptacle, preferably a graduated half-pint (10 ounce) measure. To check that the whole of the old oil is drained off, work the forks up and down sharply. Very carefully note the exact quantity of oil removed.

Using for convenience a suitable oiler, pour into each fork leg through the top screw hole approximately *one-third* of a pint (6½-7 fluid ounces, or 198 c.c.) of one of the following lubricants: Castrol XL, Essolube 30, B.P. Energol (SAE 30), Shell X100-30, Mobiloil A. If your Ariel is used for heavy sidecar duty, a somewhat heavier grade of oil can to advantage be inserted. Be most careful not to over-fill the front fork legs, otherwise some retardation of the hydraulic action is likely. After filling both fork legs, replace the plugs (*A*, Fig. 21), and tighten them firmly.

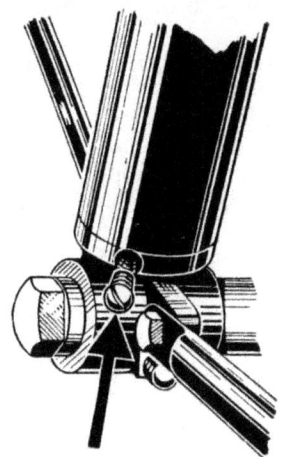

FIG. 41. FRONT FORK DRAIN PLUG
Applicable to 1954–60 "Colts"

On 1947–55 "Magdyno" Models. Note that on pre-1956 models two hexagon plugs are provided at the top of the fork legs, and these must be removed for checking the oil level and topping up. The correct oil level is 17–18 in. below the top face of the top bracket, with the motor-cycle unloaded in an upright position. This is equivalent to approximately one-third of a pint in each fork leg. Although topping up is normally unnecessary, it is desirable to check the oil level at long intervals and after dismantling and replenishing the telescopic forks. To check the oil level in each fork leg, remove the top plug and insert a dip-stick about 24 in. long through the plug hole. Any loss indicates leakage, and appropriate topping up should be undertaken.

Draining and Refilling Front Forks (1954–60 "Colts"). Every 10,000 miles, remove the hexagon-headed cap (*A*, Fig. 81) from the top of each telescopic-fork leg, using the special tool-kit spanner. Next unscrew the drain plug (shown arrowed in Fig. 41) from the bottom of each front-fork leg. Drain off the whole of the old oil; to facilitate the process, stand astride your Ariel, grasp the handlebars, and work the telescopic forks sharply up and down a few times. Using for convenience a small funnel, pour into each fork leg through the top-cap hole a quarter of a pint* of one of the following oils: Essolube 20, B.P. Energol SAE 20W, Castrol Castrolite, Shell X100 Motor Oil 20/20W, Mobiloil Arctic. Afterwards replace the hexagon-headed caps on top of the fork legs and tighten them down firmly. This is important, especially as the caps anchor the fork tubes to the top yoke.

Girder-type Front Forks (1939–46). The fork-link spindles require periodic lubrication, and the grease-gun should be applied every 250–300 miles to the grease nipples for the fork spindles and the lower joint pins of the auxiliary damper-springs. Where auxiliary damper-springs are fitted, also apply a spot of oil at the point where the top anchorages of these springs pivot on the top fork spindle.

Central Stand. Apply some oil occasionally.

* In no circumstances must the front-fork legs be filled right up to the top, or they will cease to function. The addition of an amount of oil *slightly* exceeding one-quarter of a pint is not harmful.

CHAPTER V

GENERAL MAINTENANCE

THE routine maintenance dismantling, and assembling of 1939–60 single-cylinder four-stroke Ariels is included in this chapter. Attend to maintenance regularly, and do not wait until the machine "calls out" for attention! To enable you to turn quickly to the specific instructions you need, this chapter has been subdivided into a number of main sections. All detailed references to carburation, the lighting system, and lubrication have been omitted, as these subjects have already been fully covered in Chapters II to IV.

Spares and Repairs. It is essential when you have occasion to forward or deliver parts to the manufacturers or to Ariel repair specialists (either for repair or as patterns) to attach to *each* part a label on which is written clearly your full name and address. To ensure quick attention, all correspondence concerning spares and technical advice should be written on separate sheets, each bearing your name and address.

Always quote the *complete* engine number or frame number, according to the nature of the part involved. The frame number and engine number (with letter prefix) will be found as stated in the footnote on page 1.

There are numerous firms in the United Kingdom who can supply Ariel spares over the counter, and also many who specialize in the repair of engines and gearboxes. Useful addresses may be found in the advertisement pages of the *Motor Cycle* and *Motor Cycling*. If taking a machine to Ariel Motors, Ltd., Selly Oak, Birmingham, 29, first make an appointment.

Some Large Accessory Firms. Among reputable London firms (some of which have provincial branches) handling motor-cycle accessories, equipment, proprietary spares, tools, clothing, etc., may be mentioned: Whitbys of Acton, Ltd.; Claude Rye Ltd.; E. S. Motors; The Halford Cycle Co., Ltd.; Turner's Stores; James Grose, Ltd.; Marble Arch Motor Supplies, Ltd.; Pride & Clarke, Ltd.; George Grose, Ltd.; and Kays of Ealing, Ltd.

Items Needed for Maintenance. Some items, in addition to the standard tool kit, will be needed for maintenance, and they should be kept handy in the lock-up or garage. These include: a can of paraffin for cleaning purposes; a stiff brush for scouring dirt from beneath the crankcase and gearbox; a tin of suitable engine oil for the engine and gearbox (*see* page 58); a small funnel for topping up the oil tank and gearbox; a canister of grease for replenishing the grease-gun (*see* page 73); a large drip-tray for placing beneath the engine (also necessary when draining the oil tank and sump); a medium-size galvanized pail for washing parts with paraffin; some non-fluffy rags; a fairly broad, blunt screwdriver for chipping off carbon deposits; a tin of valve-grinding paste such as Richford's (coarse and fine); a set of engine gaskets. You should also have available: a pair of new gudgeon-pin circlips; a small pair of snipe-nose pliers (for removing and fitting circlips); a pair of medium-size cutting pliers; a good make of adjustable spanner; a six-inch steel rule; a small electrical screwdriver; a valve-spring compressor (*see* page 104) for removing the valves; a suction-type valve grinding tool (*see* page 106). A gudgeon-pin extractor may also prove very useful (*see* page 101), and it is desirable to obtain a wire brush for cleaning the sparking plug, and a set of feeler gauges for checking tappet clearances, plug gap, etc., also a plug re-gapping tool (*see* page 81).

For the maintenance of the motor-cycle parts you should obtain: a tyre-pressure gauge (such as the Dunlop pencil-type No. 6, the Romac, the Schrader No. 7750, or the Holdtite), a box of spare chain-links; a chain-rivet extractor; an extractor for the clutch centre, a Lucas battery filler (*see* page 36); a hydrometer for occasionally checking the specific gravity of the battery electrolyte (*see* page 37); a chamois leather; a couple of sponges and a pail (if a hose is not available) for washing down; some soft dusters (preferably of the Selvyt type); a tin of good wax or other polish for the enamelled parts; and a tin of really good hand cleanser.

Cleanliness is Important. Keep your mount nice and clean. Doubtless it cost quite a sum, and it is well worth careful looking after. With regular and proper cleaning it will function better, will last longer, maintain its good looks, and retain a good market value. A dirty motor-cycle is an eyesore, and remember that dirt hides defects, encourages rusting, and is a menace when stripping down. Never leave your Ariel soaking wet overnight. If you have no time for cleaning in wet weather, grease the machine all over *before* use.

Cleaning the Engine and Gearbox. See that the cylinder barrel and cylinder-head fins are kept clean and black (except aluminium alloy heads). If the enamel has worn away, paint the fins with some proprietary cylinder black after thorough cleaning with a stiff brush dipped in paraffin. Note that rusted fins, besides looking shabby, cause an appreciable loss in heat dispersion.

Scour off all filth from the lower part of the engine and gearbox with stiff brushes and paraffin. Clean all aluminium alloy and bright surfaces first with a rag damped in paraffin, assisted by brushes where necessary, and then with a dry rag.

Cleaning the Enamel. Never attempt to remove mud from the enamelled parts when dry and caked, as this is likely to damage the surfaces. Soak the mud off with a hose if available. In the case of a very dirty machine it may be advisable to paint the surfaces over with a cleaning compound such as "Gunk" before directing a stream of water on to the dirty surfaces. Be careful not to allow any water to get on the wheel-hub bearings, and the "Magdyno" and carburettor. If a hose is not available, soak the mud and then disperse it with plenty of clean water, using a sponge and pail.

Having removed all dirt, dry the enamelled surfaces with a chamois leather and afterwards polish them with soft dusters and some good wax polish or a proprietary polish such as "Karpol."

"Dry weather" riders can keep a machine in almost showroom condition merely by rubbing the enamel over with a paraffin-damped rag, followed by a dry, soft duster.

Cleaning the Chromium. Never employ liquid metal polish or paste, as this will wear down the thin surface. A good chromium-cleaning compound can, however, safely be used, though too frequent use is not desirable. The normal method of removing tarnish (salt deposits) is to clean the surfaces regularly with a damp chamois leather and then polish them with soft dusters.

To Reduce Tarnishing. During the winter months it is a good plan to wipe over occasionally all chromium surfaces with a soft cloth soaked in a proprietary anti-tarnish preparation. An example is "Tekall," obtainable in ½-pint and 1-pint tins.

Regularly Check Nuts for Tightness. This is particularly important during running-in (*see* page 17), as some "bedding down" of parts occurs. Regularly apply spanners to the various external nuts to ensure tightness, paying special attention to the engine bolts and nuts, the engine mounting nuts, and the pipe unions. After running-in, check them about every 2,000 miles, but after decarbonizing and running for about 250 miles, check the cylinder-head bolts for tightness, tightening them diagonally.

Carburettor Tuning, Maintenance. For detailed instructions, *see* Chapter II.

Lubrication. Detailed instructions for the lubrication of 1939 and later Ariels are given in Chapter IV, and the lubrication location chart on page 70 shows where the application of grease or oil is mainly required.

CARE OF THE IGNITION SYSTEM

In this section the Wipac alternator and battery (used for lighting and ignition on the 200 c.c. coil-ignition "Colts") are not dealt with, these components having already been covered in Chapter IV which discusses the lighting system. The ignition switch on coil-ignition models is referred to on page 5.

Recommended Sparking Plugs. To ensure easy starting, a cool-running engine and good all-round performance, it is essential always to run on a type of sparking plug recommended by the engine manufacturers. Three reliable and recommended makes are the Lodge, the K.L.G., and the Champion. Waterproof terminal covers, watertight plugs, and "ignition-suppression" (*see* page 3) sparking plugs are available.

Suitable Lodge Types. On all 1939–51 S.V. engines requiring 14 mm sparking plugs fit a Lodge CN or CI4. On the 1952–4 S.V. engines fit a Lodge CLNH or CB14 plug, and on the 1955–8 S.V. engines a Lodge HLN.

On all O.H.V. engines (including "Colt" engines) requiring a 14 mm sparking plug, fit a Lodge HLN, except in two cases: On Model VH up to 1952 a Lodge CN or C14 is recommended; on Model NH up to 1955 fit a Lodge HN or H14. On earlier type O.H.V. engines requiring an 18 mm plug, fit a Lodge H3 sparking plug.

Suitable Champion and K.L.G. Types. If you prefer to fit a Champion or K.L.G. sparking plug as an alternative to the Lodge plug, fit the appropriate type as indicated in the accompanying cross-reference chart (Table V).

TABLE V

SPARKING-PLUG CROSS-REFERENCE CHART

Lodge Plug	Champion Plug	K.L.G. Plug	Diameter (mm)	Reach (in.)
CN	L10	F50	14	$\frac{1}{2}$
CI4	L10	F50	14	$\frac{1}{2}$
CLNH	N8	FE50	14	$\frac{3}{4}$
CB14	N8	FE30	14	$\frac{3}{4}$
HLN	N5	FE70	14	$\frac{3}{4}$
HN	L7	F70	14	$\frac{1}{2}$
H14	L7	F70	14	$\frac{1}{2}$
H3	K11, 17	M60	18	$\frac{1}{2}$

The Sparking Plug Gap. Difficult starting or occasional misfiring can usually be traced to a dirty or unserviceable sparking plug. The life of a good plug is considerable, but the points of the electrodes gradually burn away and eventually the gap becomes too large and it is necessary to reset the points.

It is advisable to check the plug gap regularly (say every 2,500 miles) and to adjust the gap on "Magdyno" models if burning of the points has

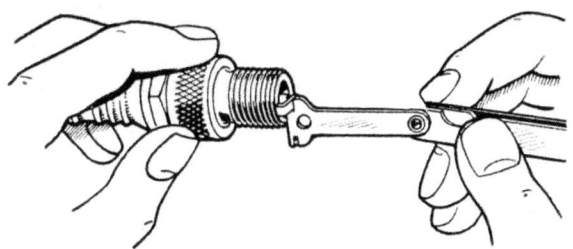

Fig. 42. A Safe Method of Re-gapping a Plug
The Champion tool shown includes suitable gauges

caused the gap to exceed 0·022 in. Ariel Motors, Ltd. recommend a gap of 0·018–0·022 in. (0·020 in.–0·030 in.* on coil-ignition models). For obvious reasons, when re-gapping it is advisable to set the gap at or near the *bottom* limit. Check the gap with a suitable feeler gauge. The gauge should just enter without springing the points.

When adjusting the plug gap, never attempt to bend or tap the *centre* electrode. Use a pair of snipe-nose pliers, or a plug re-gapping tool (shown in Fig. 42), to bend the outside (earth) electrode(s). Tapping the earth electrode(s) is not a good method. When the plug has to be thoroughly cleaned, this should be done as described below, and the plug re-gapped *afterwards*.

Cleaning the Plug. If carburation is correct and excessive oil is not entering the combustion chamber, it should not be necessary to dismantle and clean the sparking plug thoroughly more often than once about every 3,000 miles. When running-in a new or rebored engine, it is advisable to remove and check the plug for cleanliness at intervals of about 500 miles.

Quick cleaning of a plug can be done by brushing the points and slightly rubbing their firing sides with smooth emery-cloth. Alternatively the plug

---

* On coil-ignition models the plug gap can often be safely increased to as much as 0·035 in., the limit being set by possible misfiring at high speeds. Where an "ignition suppression" type plug or terminal cover is fitted, the plug-gap should not be less than 0·025 in. This applies to both coil- and magneto ignition models.

can be cleaned with a proprietary gadget. Thorough cleaning (internal and external), however, is not possible without dismantling the plug.

To Clean K.L.G. and Lodge Plugs Thoroughly. Fig. 43 shows a typical detachable type (K.L.G.) sparking plug dismantled for thorough cleaning.

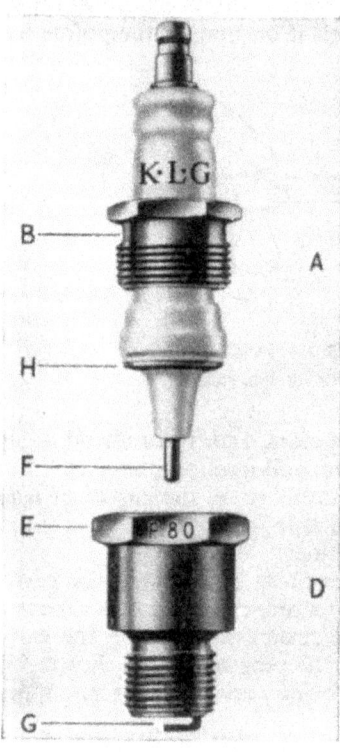

Fig. 43. Detachable-type Sparking Plug (K.L.G.) Dismantled for Thorough Cleaning

The gland nut *B* and the internal washer *H* are shown still in position on the insulation

To dismantle a detachable-type sparking plug, hold the smaller hexagon of the gland nut (B) lightly in a vice or with a suitable spanner. If you use a vice, be most careful not to exert any pressure on the hexagon faces. Then with a suitable box spanner applied to the larger hexagon (E) of the plug body, unscrew the body until it is separated from the gland nut.* The centre electrode (F) with its insulation (comprising the insulated electrode assembly (A)) can now be detached from the gland nut. Take care not to lose the internal sealing washer (H).

To clean the insulation, wipe it clean with a cloth soaked in petrol or paraffin. If the insulation is coated with hard-carbon deposits, remove these with some fine emery-cloth, but make no attempt to scrape off the deposits. The internal sealing washer (H) and the surfaces on the insulator, and in the metal body on which this washer rests, are very important as they prevent gas leakage through the plug. Therefore wipe them only with a rag soaked in petrol or paraffin. Any damage caused while dismantling will render the plug unserviceable.

To clean the metal parts (plug body and gland nut) wipe them clean with petrol, or, if necessary, scrape off the deposits with a small knife, or use a wire brush. Afterwards rinse the parts in petrol. The gland nut seldom gets very fouled, but the inside of the plug body may be very dirty, and the same may apply to the external threads of the plug. Clean

* Where a detachable-type sparking plug has been in service for a very considerable time, the plug may be found extremely difficult to dismantle, in which case the attempt should be abandoned.

and polish the points of the centre and outside (earth) electrodes (*F*) and (*G*) (Fig. 43) with some fine emery cloth.

See that there is no dirt or grit lodged between the body of the plug and the insulation, and particularly on the internal sealing washer and the contacting faces. Smear a little thin oil on the internal washer and make sure that it seats properly. When assembling the sparking plug, see that the centre electrode and insulation are positioned centrally in the body bore. If they are not, remove, re-position by rotating assembly (*A*) a quarter of a turn, and reassemble. Do not attempt to force it into position or bend it.

Avoid excessive tightening of the gland nut (*B*). Finally verify that the plug gap is correct (*see* page 81).

Cleaning Champion Plugs. To clean a non-detachable type Champion plug, take it to the nearest garage equipped with a Champion Service Unit. With this apparatus the plug can be cleaned of all deposits in a few minutes, washed, subjected to a high-pressure air line, and afterwards tested for sparking on the Champion apparatus at an air pressure of over 100 lb per sq in.

Replacing the Plug. Before replacing a plug, renew the copper washer if it is worn or flattened, and clean the plug threads with a wire brush. Screw the plug home by hand as far as possible, and always use the plug spanner for final tightening.

When replacing a sparking plug on a light-alloy cylinder head, smear the threads with graphite and do not over-tighten or difficulty may be experienced in removing the plug after carbon has been deposited around the threads.

Lubrication of Lucas "Magdyno," or Wipac Contact-breaker. For appropriate instructions, *see* Chapter III, pages 67-9.

Testing the Plug and H.T. Cable. The usual method of testing for H.T. current at the plug terminal is to bridge the terminal and the cylinder head with the steel blade of a *wooden-handled* screwdriver, when a spark should be visible on rotating the engine. To test the plug itself, remove it with the H.T. lead attached, clean it, lay it on the cylinder (with the terminal clear of the head) and ascertain whether it sparks satisfactorily with the engine rotated with the kick-starter. In daylight the spark is not bright, but it should be distinctly heard.

Lucas "Magdyno" Contact-breaker Gap. Little attention to the ignition portion of the Lucas "Magdyno" is needed, other than occasional lubrication (*see* page 67) and attention to the face-cam type contact-breaker, shown in Fig. 44. Any serious internal trouble should be dealt with by a Lucas service agent.

The contacts of the contact-breaker (Fig. 44) should be examined on a new machine after the first 500 miles, and subsequently about every 3,000 miles. If the "break," with the contacts full open is appreciably more, or less, than will just hold a 0·012 in.–0·015 in. blade of a feeler gauge the

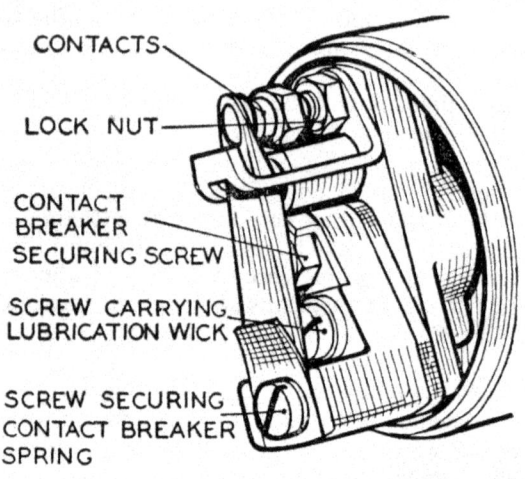

Fig. 44. The Face-cam Type Contact-breaker on the Lucas "Magdyno" (1939 Onwards)

contacts should be adjusted (*after* cleaning, if necessary). Too great a gap will advance the timing. The magneto-spanner gauge or the blade of a proprietary set of feelers, can be useful for checking the "break," the procedure for which is as follows—

1. Remove the contact-breaker cover and rotate the engine slowly forwards until the contacts of the contact-breaker are wide open (i.e. near T.D.C. on the compression stroke).

2. Insert the blade of the feeler gauge between the contacts.

3. If the feeler gauge *just* slides in without friction, the gap is correct and no adjustment is needed. If the gauge is a slack fit or the contacts have to be sprung to enable it to enter, adjust the gap as below.

4. With the magneto spanner loosen the lock-nut which secures the adjustable-contact screw (*see* Fig. 44) and then adjust this screw by means of its hexagon head until the correct gap is obtained between the fixed and movable contacts.

5. Retighten the contact screw lock-nut and again check the gap. If correct, replace the contact-breaker cover.

GENERAL MAINTENANCE

Wipac Contact-breaker (1954–60 "Colts"). On a new 200 c.c. "Colt" check the gap between the contact points of the contact-breaker after covering 500 miles, and then at intervals of about 2,000 miles. To obtain access to the contacts it is only necessary to remove the contact-breaker cover, which is incidentally the Ariel "Colt" name-plate (*see* Fig. 64). If the "break," with the contacts wide open, is appreciably more, or less, than

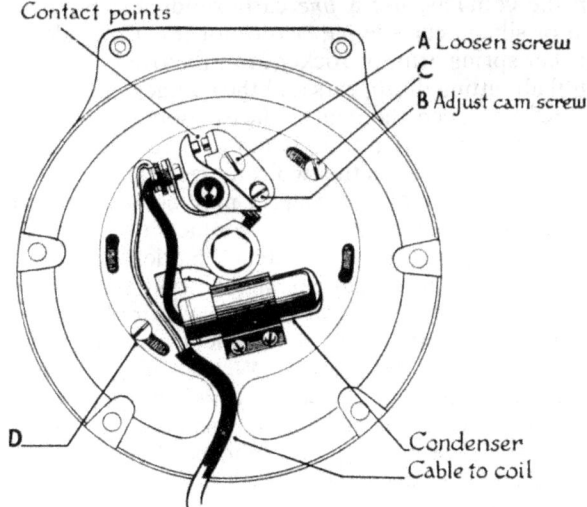

FIG. 45. THE WIPAC CONTACT-BREAKER AND MOUNTING PLATE
Applies to 1954 and later "Colts"

will just hold a 0·012 in.–0·015 in. blade of a feeler gauge, the contact points should be adjusted (after cleaning, if necessary).

To adjust the contact-breaker contacts, turn the engine (with the sparking plug removed) until the contact rocker-arm fibre heel is positioned on the centre of the operating cam (*see* Fig. 45). Loosen the lock-screw (*A*) and then turn the small cam-screw (*B*) clockwise to increase the gap, or anti-clockwise to decrease it. Afterwards check the gap accurately with a feeler gauge and securely tighten screw (*A*).

Cleaning the Contact-breaker Contacts. At intervals of about 2,000 or 3,000 miles, when checking the contact-breaker gap, scrutinize the contacts closely. If the contacts are allowed to become dirty or oily, rapid burning, pitting, and consequent ignition trouble will ensue.

If inspection reveals that the contacts have a *grey, frosted* appearance, with no blackening or pitting, do not interfere with them (assuming that the gap is correct). If the contacts are only slightly discoloured, clean them with a thin cloth moistened with petrol.

On examination after a big mileage the contacts may be found to have irregular and blackened areas due to pitting and burning (especially if the contacts have not been kept clean and correctly adjusted). In this case it is essential to clean them up, otherwise misfiring and rapid deterioration of the contacts will probably follow.

To clean the contacts, use a *fine* carborundum slip or a piece of *fine* emery cloth or silicon-carbide paper (do not use a nail file), and with the contact-breaker spring arm, or rocker arm, removed, clean and polish the contacts until all pitting disappears and the contact surfaces are smooth all over. Be careful to keep the contact faces "square" as well as uniform. *This is most important.** If pitting is not appreciable it is permissible to insert the emery cloth between the two contacts, while both are in position. If pitting is very substantial and deep, it may be necessary to remove the complete contact-breaker to restore the contacts to serviceable condition. Always remove the spring arm ("Magdyno" models) first, and remove any traces of rust from it. Note that it is highly inadvisable to remove much metal from the contact faces. Always fit a new pair of contacts (including, of course, a new spring arm) if a reasonable amount of facing-up fails to renovate the contacts satisfactorily. When fitting a new spring arm ("Magdyno"), make sure that the spring arm is properly located (*see* next paragraph). After trueing up the contacts as described above, be careful to remove all metal dust with a petrol-moistened cloth, and do not forget to check the contact-breaker gap which will have increased if much pitting has been eliminated.

To Remove the Spring Arm (Lucas "Magdyno"). To remove the spring arm (carrying the moving contact) on the face-cam type contact-breaker (*see* Fig. 44), it is only necessary to remove its securing screw and spring washer. When replacing the spring arm, make certain that the small backing spring is replaced immediately under the securing screw and spring washer, with the curved portion facing *outwards* as shown in Fig. 44. See that the contacts are perfectly aligned before firmly tightening the securing screw.

It is desirable at long intervals to remove the complete contact-breaker and inspect the small fibre tappet which operates the spring arm. If its edges are at all worn, renew the tappet immediately. Smear a little thin machine oil on the tappet before fitting it to the contact-breaker body.

To remove the complete contact-breaker after detaching the spring arm, unlock the tab-washer and remove the contact-breaker securing screw, when the complete contact-breaker can be withdrawn, and dealt with on a

---

* On some later type "Magdyno" contact-breakers the contact faces of the contacts are slightly convex, not flat, and emery cloth must therefore be used to clean them.

bench or table if desired. When replacing the contact-breaker, see that a new tab-washer is fitted and locked over the securing screw.

The Automatic Advance Mechanism (1954-60 "Colts"). Behind the contact-breaker is the automatic-advance mechanism (*see* Fig. 54). It positions the cam automatically and advances the spark as the speed of the engine increases. *Normally the mechanism requires no attention,* but should occasion arise to dismantle the unit, examine the action of the governor controls and check that they work freely. Wipe the controls clean, and well lubricate with some thin cycle oil.

The Ignition Control. On 200 c.c. "Colts" the coil is oil-filled to assist cooling. To inspect the terminals (which must be absolutely clean and free from corrosion), remove the top cover by unscrewing the two slotted brass nuts at the top. The remainder of the coil unit is sealed during initial assembly, and do not tamper with it.

The Rectifier. For instructions, *see* page 47.

VALVE CLEARANCES

It is very important to maintain the correct valve clearances on all Ariel engines, and the clearances should be checked about every 1,000 miles when the engine is *quite cold*; after 250 miles in the case of new engines where considerable "bedding down" of the parts occurs; after grinding-in the valves. It should be noted that incorrect valve clearances interfere with both the lift of the valves and also the valve timing.

TABLE VI

CORRECT VALVE CLEARANCES (ENGINE COLD)

Engine Type	Inlet Valve	Exhaust Valve
(M) 1939–50 S.V.	0·002 in.	0·004 in.
1951–8 S.V.	0·003 in.	0·006 in.
1939–50 O.H.V.	Nil	Nil
1951–3 O.H.V.	Nil	0·002 in.
1954–60 O.H.V.	0·006 in.	0·008 in.
(C) 1954–5 O.H.V. ("Colt")	0·001 in.	0·002 in.
1956–60 O.H.V. ("Colt")	0·010 in.	0·012 in.

Note. The abbreviations (M) and (C) indicate "Magdyno" and coil-ignition equipped engines respectively. It is assumed that the valve timing is correct.

Excessive clearances result in reduced valve lift and late opening of the valves which cause undue noise and loss of efficiency, but this is not likely to damage the valves. Insufficient valve clearances, besides resulting in loss of compression, flexibility, and power, may cause distortion and perhaps burning of the exhaust valve due to gas leakage past it during the power strokes. Experienced riders can usually tell by the sound and "feel" of an engine whether the valve clearances are correct. Before checking the valve clearances it is essential to set the piston at top-dead-centre and then check that there is sufficient clearance at the exhaust-valve lifter. Check the exhaust-valve lifter adjustment again *after* checking the valve clearances.

FIG. 46. TAPPET ADJUSTMENT (1939–58 S.V.)

To Adjust Tappets (All 1939–58 S.V. Engines). Remove the valve-chest cover and set the engine with the piston somewhere near the top of the cylinder with the valves fully closed. Referring to Fig. 46, to adjust each tappet, the tappet (C) should be held while the lock-nut (B) is loosened. Then rotate (A), holding the tappet (C) until the desired clearance is obtained. Now secure the lock-nut (B) and recheck the clearance several times whilst rotating the engine from the position where the inlet valve closes until the exhaust valve opens.

On all Ariel S.V. engines the clearance is measured with a feeler gauge between the top of the tappet head and the end of the valve stem. Do not be confused by there being no clearance for a few degrees just as each valve opens and closes; this is due to the action of the cam taking up the clearance slowly before the valves begin to open.

Adjusting Valve Clearances (1939–53 O.H.V.). On 1939–53 O.H.V. Ariel engines ("Magdyno" models) the overhead rocker adjustment (*see* Fig. 47) is enclosed by quickly-detachable hexagon-headed caps. Loosen these with a spanner and remove by hand. Prior to adjusting the valve clearances, set the engine with both valves *fully closed* and the piston at the top of the compression stroke.

To make each valve clearance adjustment, loosen the lock-nut on the adjuster screw which passes through the outer end of the rocker arm and bears on the hardened valve stem end-cap. Now rotate the adjuster screw until the valve clearance is correct, and then re-tighten the lock-nut. Make

GENERAL MAINTENANCE 89

sure that the overhead-rocker return spring is keeping the inner end of the rocker in full contact with the push-rod. Where the exhaust rocker is concerned, make quite certain that there is sufficient backlash at the exhaust-valve lifter (*see* page 92) *before* checking the clearance of the exhaust valve.

Where the valve clearance is *nil* (*see* Table VI) a practical way of checking that the adjustment is correct is to verify that it is impossible to depress

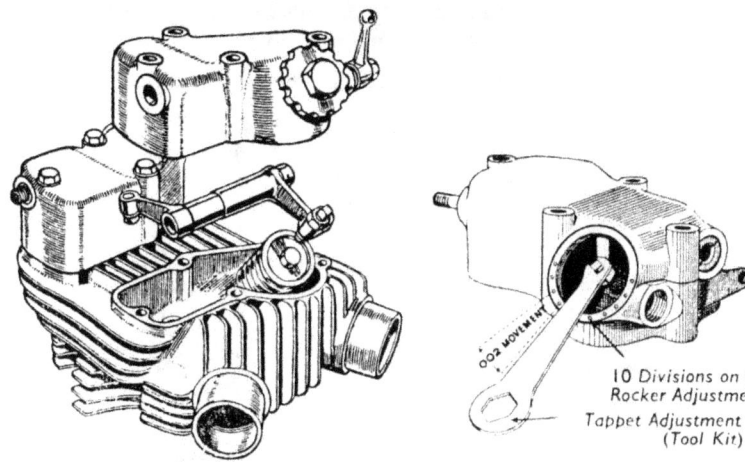

FIG. 47. ROCKER-BOX COMPONENTS ON TYPICAL 1950 O.H.V. ENGINE
(*By courtesy of "Motor Cycle," London*)

FIG. 48. VALVE CLEARANCE ADJUSTMENT (1954–5 O.H.V.)
Not applicable to 200 c.c. "Colt" engines

the end of the rocker arm, and then to test the compression of the engine. If satisfactory results are obtained it can be assumed that the valve concerned is seating properly. If the engine lacks good compression, either a valve is being held off its seat through too close an adjustment, or there is serious leakage elsewhere. In either case the cause must be found and rectified.

To Adjust Valve Clearances (1954–5 O.H.V.). To guarantee accurate adjustment, the rocker-boxes ("Magdyno" models) have their screw-cap joint rims marked with indentations, each representing 0·002 in. movement of the adjuster screw (*see* Fig. 48). By holding the tappet spanner against the joint rim, each separate 0·002 in. movement can be *felt* and it is not difficult to obtain the correct valve clearance by carefully moving the spanner. On the 1954–5 O.H.V. engines check that there is sufficient backlash at the exhaust-valve lifter before making an adjustment, but do not set the engine so that the piston is exactly at T.D.C., with both valves fully closed.

Rotate the engine slowly in its normal direction of rotation until the exhaust valve is just beginning to lift, and then adjust the clearance of the *inlet* valve (0·006 in.). Having correctly adjusted the clearance of the inlet valve, further rotate the engine slowly forward until the inlet valve just closes, and then proceed to check the clearance of the *exhaust* valve (0·008 in.).

When making a valve clearance adjustment, always first turn the adjuster screw (after slackening the lock-nut) *clockwise* to give just *nil* clearance,

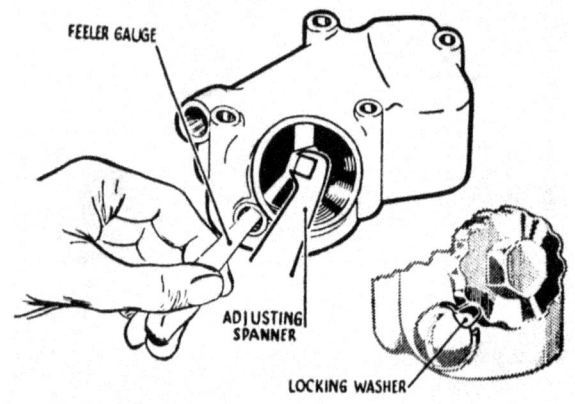

Fig. 49. Valve Clearance Adjustment (1956–60 O.H.V.)
Not applicable to 200 c.c. "Colt" engines

and then unscrew the adjuster *anti-clockwise* to obtain the correct valve clearance. Afterwards firmly tighten the lock-nut which secures the adjuster screw, and replace the rocker-box cap. Deal with each valve similarly.

Adjusting Valve Clearances (1956–60 O.H.V.). On 1956–9 O.H.V. Ariels with "Magdyno" ignition and lighting equipment, to ensure accurate valve clearance adjustment each rocker assembly is quickly accessible on removing the large screwed cap, and a smaller screwed plug, as shown in Fig. 49.

On removing the smaller plug an aperture is exposed to enable a feeler gauge to be inserted as shown, so that it is positioned between the rocker adjusting screw and the valve stem or valve stem end-cap (when fitted). By this method an accurate check of the valve clearance (*see* Table VI) can be made for each valve.

The correct procedure for checking and adjusting the inlet- and exhaust-valve clearances is identical with that stated in the preceding section (excluding the first paragraph) dealing with 1954–5 O.H.V. engines.

To Adjust Valve Clearances (1954–60 O.H.V. "Colts"). On the 200 c.c. coil-ignition models first detach the rocker-box cover after removing the single bolt securing its centre to the rocker-box. When removing the cover be careful not to damage the gasket, otherwise a new gasket will be required on assembly to avoid the risk of oil leakage. Remove the 14 mm sparking plug and then rotate the engine until the piston is at top-dead-centre (T.D.C.) on the compression stroke. To find the true T.D.C. position,

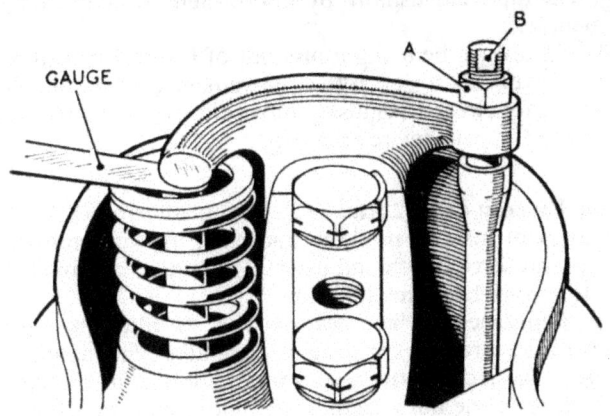

FIG. 50. VALVE CLEARANCE ADJUSTMENT (1954–60 O.H.V. "COLTS")
See also sectional view on page 99

insert a length of stout wire through the sparking plug hole. When no movement of the wire can be felt on "rocking" the engine slightly backwards and forwards, the piston is at T.D.C. In this position both valves are fully closed.

Referring to Fig. 50, to check and adjust each valve clearance, apply a small fixed spanner to the flats on the adjuster pin (*B*) and while holding the adjuster pin quite stationary, loosen the lock-nut (*A*) with the tappet spanner provided in the tool kit. Again hold the lock-nut (*A*) stationary and screw the adjuster pin (*B*) in or out as required until the correct feeler gauge (*see* Table VI) just enters the gap between the rocker arm and the valve stem as shown in Fig. 50. Then while preventing any further movement of the adjuster pin, firmly tighten the lock-nut (*A*) against the rocker arm.

Having adjusted the valve clearance and secured the adjuster pin, again check the clearance in case any movement of the adjuster pin has occurred while tightening the lock-nut. Replace the 14 mm sparking plug and fit the gasket and rocker-box cover. To avoid oil leakage, the gasket must be in perfect condition, assuming that the old gasket is being fitted.

Exhaust-valve Lifter Adjustment (S.V. and O.H.V.). An exhaust-valve lifter is provided on all models except the 1954–60 200 c.c. "Colt" engines. Before checking the valve clearances as previously described, and at all other times, it is most important that there should not be an entire absence of backlash at the exhaust-valve lifter lever with the exhaust valve fully closed. Absence of backlash prevents the exhaust valve from seating properly, and this causes loss of compression and burning of the valve and its seating, accompanied usually by intermittent banging in the exhaust pipe and silencer.

There should always be a slight amount of lost motion (about $\frac{1}{8}$ in.) in the operating lever or trigger before movement of the control (with the exhaust valve fully closed) begins to move the tappet or overhead rocker on S.V. and O.H.V. engines respectively.

To Adjust Exhaust-valve Lifter (S.V.). On all Ariel S.V. engines the desired adjustment may be made by loosening the lock-nut on the cable adjuster stop and screwing the adjuster in or out as required a few turns. After adjusting re-tighten the lock-nut.

A further adjustment, where necessary, is to alter the setting of the exhaust-valve lifter arm on the eccentric spindle. This is only held by a nut and taper. To slack off the taper joint, undo the nut a couple of turns, and give the face of the nut a light, sharp blow, so as to drive the spindle inwards. Set the arm as described below and re-tighten the nut.

The additional adjustment can be made by altering the position of the exhaust-valve lifter arm on its spindle as follows. With cable connected, rotate the engine until the inlet and exhaust valves are shut. Then release the spindle arm as described in the paragraph already given above. Now move the exhaust-valve lifter lever or trigger (on the handlebars) until the end of the lifter arm has moved forward about $\frac{1}{4}$ in. from its normal "Off" position. Next with a screwdriver applied to the slot in the spindle end, turn the spindle in an *anti-clockwise* direction until the lifter arm contacts the collar on the tappet. In this position tighten the lock-nut securely. Make quite certain that the crank on the inner end of the spindle is not contacting the collar of the exhaust tappet, with the exhaust-valve lifter out of action.

To Adjust Exhaust-valve Lifter (O.H.V.). Contrary to the arrangement on S.V. engines, there is no adjustment provided on 1939–60 O.H.V. engines for the control cable itself.

To adjust the exhaust-valve lifter, it is necessary to alter the setting of the exhaust-valve lifter arm on its eccentric spindle. To do this, first slacken the taper joint between the spindle and arm by undoing the securing nut a few turns. Then direct a light but sharp blow on the nut face. This should drive the spindle inwards.

GENERAL MAINTENANCE

Do not disconnect the central cable. Rotate the engine until both valves are closed. Then operate the control on the handlebars until the top end of the lifter arm has moved forward about $\frac{1}{4}$ in. from the "Off" position. Now turn the lifter spindle *clockwise*, by means of a screwdriver applied to the slotted spindle-end, until the lifter arm contacts the rocker on the left-hand side of the rocker-box, looking from the rear. Afterwards firmly tighten the lock-nut. Also verify that the lifter arm has slight idle movement before it contacts the overhead rocker with valve closed. It should be noted that turning the eccentric spindle clockwise or anti-clockwise decreases or increases the clearance between the overhead rocker arm and the lifter arm.

DECARBONIZING AND VALVE GRINDING

The removal of carbon deposits is generally only necessary when the engine displays a tendency to run hot, and when certain characteristic symptoms (*see* below) become manifest. Under normal running conditions decarbonizing should only be undertaken after the first 1,500 miles and thereafter at periods exceeding 3,000 miles, and not till the engine *really needs it*. Valve grinding may be needed when decarbonizing, and the valves and their seats should always be inspected. Valve removal facilitates cleaning the ports. Certain items required for the complete maintenance operation are mentioned on page 77.

The cylinder barrel should also be removed at every alternate decarbonizing and the piston and rings inspected. The big- and small-end bearings can be checked for wear at the same time. Decarbonizing is very simple, and it is not necessary to remove the cylinder barrel during each "top overhaul" because most of the carbon deposits form on the piston crown, which is accessible on removing the cylinder head. The necessity for decarbonizing is indicated by a gradual falling off in power (especially on hills), a tendency for "pinking" (injurious to the engine) under slight provocation, and a "woolly" exhaust. The sparking plug also tends to become dirty very quickly.

Dealing with Petrol Tank. On side-valve engines it is *not* necessary to remove the petrol tank in order to remove the cylinder head, and also the cylinder barrel where considered necessary. The general accessibility on a S.V. engine is obviously superior to that on an overhead-valve engine because on the O.H.V. type the upper part of the cylinder head includes a rocker-box or rocker-boxes in very close proximity to the frame top-tube. Some riders, however, prefer always to remove the petrol tank when decarbonizing any engine.

On all O.H.V. engines the petrol tank should be removed before attempting to strip-down for decarbonizing, and there are several different ways of removing the tank, depending on the model concerned and the date of manufacture. Appropriate instructions are given in the following numbered paragraphs.

1. 1957–60 "Magdyno" Models. A single-bolt fixing to the frame top-tube is provided for the petrol tank on all 1957–60 "Magdyno" models with "swinging arm" rear suspension, and this design renders tank removal and replacement, when decarbonizing, extremely simple.

To take off the petrol tank, first disconnect the petrol pipe and also remove the two small securing-screws from the front end of the chromium-

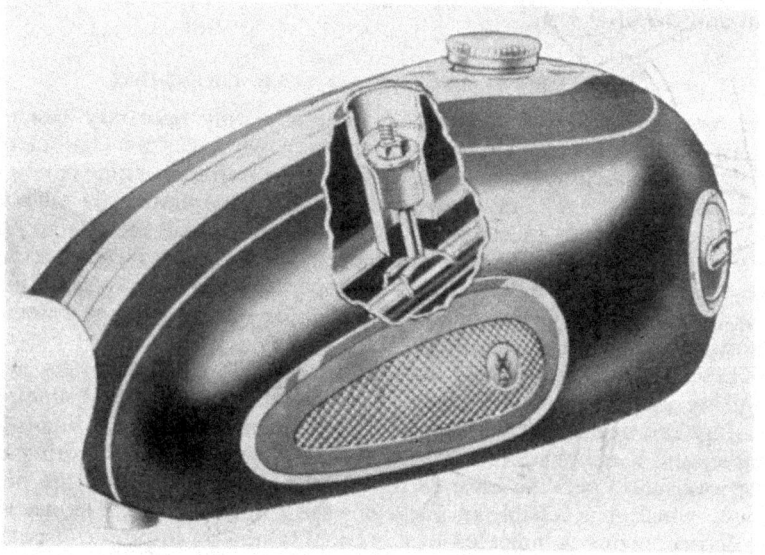

Fig. 51. The Modified Petrol Tank with Single-bolt Fixing
(1957–60 "Magdyno" Models)

Applicable to S.V. and O.H.V. Ariels, but not to O.H.V. "Colt" engines with coil ignition

plated strip across the top face of the tank, and withdraw the strip. Note the method of attachment at the rear end. Next with a suitable box spanner, inserted through the centre orifice of the tank, remove the nut from the single fixing-bolt (*see* Fig. 51) and lift the petrol tank off the frame.

When lifting away the petrol tank be careful not to misplace the steel flat-washer and also a spring-washer located beneath the fixing-bolt nut. Observe also the position of the steel distance-tube and thick packing-rubber through which the fixing bolt is fitted. Also note the method whereby the head of the self-aligning fixing bolt is located in the slotted bracket on the frame top-tube.

GENERAL MAINTENANCE

When replacing the petrol tank make sure that the four rubber buffers are correctly positioned in the recesses provided in the base of the petrol tank. These rubber buffers, together with the rubber sleeve through which the central fixing-bolt passes, give perfect shock-absorbing qualities and ensure no vibration.

2. 1939–56 "Magdyno" Models. On most 1939–50 models an instrument panel is mounted on top of the petrol tank, and certain pipe and other connexions have to be disconnected prior to removing the tank, complete with instrument panel. On the 1951–6 models having no instrument panel, tank removal is easier.

Where an instrument panel is fitted (1939–50) first disconnect the petrol feed pipe, the oil pressure gauge pipe at the rocker-box union, and the speedometer-drive cable from the gearbox by undoing the small fixing screw in the face of the gearbox just below where the cable enters the gearbox. Pull the cable out of the box. Also remove the cross-pipe* connecting the two sides of the tank after first emptying the tank. Disconnect the two panel-lamp leads.

To remove the 1939–56 petrol tank (with or without instrument panel) now unscrew the four tank-securing set-bolts, together with their shock-absorbing rubber washers and steel washers. Note that each set-bolt has *two* rubber washers and *one* plain-steel washer. Also note that when subsequently tightening the four set-bolts, excessive tightening must be avoided.

Where an instrument panel is included, on assembly re-connect the petrol cross-pipe, the petrol-feed pipe, the oil pressure gauge pipe, the speedometer flex, and the panel-lamp leads. When inserting the speedometer flex into the gearbox, it will probably be necessary to rotate the rear wheel so that the flat metal tongue on the end of the inner cable can slip into mesh with the corresponding slot on the driving spindle.

3. 1954–60 Coil-ignition "Colts." Petrol tank removal is very straightforward. First turn off the petrol tap and disconnect the petrol pipe from the tank. The petrol tank is secured at the front to the steering-head lug, and at the rear to the frame top-tube. Remove the two fixing-bolts at the front. Each bolt has one plain washer and one spring washer. Also remove the rear fixing-bolt and nut, together with the two plain washers, the single spring-washer, and the rubber pads. Carefully note the correct positions of all these items to ensure their correct replacement.

To Remove Cylinder Head (1939–58 S.V.). It is only necessary to remove the cast-iron or light-alloy cylinder head in order to decarbonize and

---

* *Note.* As the cross-pipe comes below the petrol tank, it is liable to choke with sediment, etc. If, therefore, the petrol capacity of the tank appears to diminish, remove the pipe and clean it so that there is a free petrol flow between the two sides of the tank.

grind-in the valves. Because the valves can be removed and ground-in with the cylinder barrel in position, it is advisable not to disturb the barrel unless it is desired to inspect the piston, piston rings, and to decarbonize the ring grooves and the inside of the piston.

On 1939–51 S.V. engines with a cast-iron cylinder head, to remove the head, first remove the sparking plug and undo the seven set-bolts securing the cylinder head to the cylinder barrel. On post-1951 engines (from engine Nos. TC101 to TC225) with a light-alloy cylinder head there are nine set-bolts to be removed. On all subsequent engines with a light-alloy head, remove the sparking plug and the nine hexagon nuts and plain washers fitted to the fixed studs on the top face of the cylinder barrel (*see* Fig. 52). Afterwards lift the cylinder head clear of the cylinder barrel studs. Be careful not to damage the copper-asbestos gasket. Renew the gasket if at all damaged.

To Remove Cylinder Barrel (1939–58 S.V.). Having removed the cylinder head, proceed to remove the Amal carburettor, the breather pipe from the valve chest, the exhaust pipe, and the exhaust-valve lifter cable. Now unscrew *evenly* the four cylinder-base retaining nuts and lift the cylinder barrel carefully upwards and forwards. Push the piston down to the bottom of its stroke before removing the barrel, and the cylinder barrel will emerge clear of the piston. Cover up the crankcase mouth with a cloth.

To Remove Cylinder Head (1939–60 O.H.V. "Magdyno" Models). First remove the petrol tank (*see* page 93), the Amal carburettor, the sparking plug, and the exhaust pipe(s). The exhaust-valve lifter cable and the oil-feed pipe to the rocker-boxes should then be disconnected. Actually, it is preferable to remove this feed pipe. Then remove the two screwed-caps over the valve clearance adjusters, and turn the engine forward until the piston is at top-dead-centre and both valves are fully closed.

Next unscrew the four bolts securing each rocker-box, lift the boxes clear of the valves, and swing them outwards until it is possible to raise them clear of the push-rods. Pull out both push-rods. Having done this, undo the four cylinder-head bolts and carefully remove the cylinder head. If the joint is stiff, tap the head gently upwards with a wooden mallet or raw-hide hammer applied below the inlet and exhaust ports (not the fins) until the head is freed. Be extremely careful not to damage the cylinder-head fins (especially on a light-alloy head), and if you use a screwdriver to break the joint, do not scratch the joint faces. No cylinder-head gasket is provided as on the S.V. engines.

Removal of the cylinder head exposes the push-rod covers on all 1939–53 engines and 1954 350 c.c. engines. On the 1954–5 500 c.c. engine and all 1956–60 engines the push-rods are enclosed by cast-in channels on the cylinder barrel.

GENERAL MAINTENANCE

To Remove Cylinder Barrel (1939–60 O.H.V. "Magdyno" Models).
Having removed the rocker-boxes, cylinder head, and push-rods, remove the four (five on 1956–60 engines) cylinder-barrel base nuts. Push the

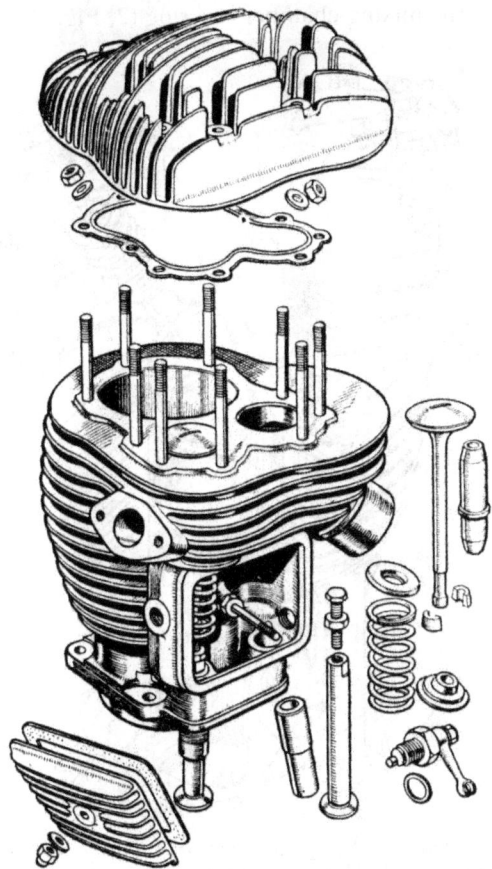

FIG. 52. DETAILS OF THE CYLINDER HEAD (LIGHT-ALLOY), THE CYLINDER BARREL, VALVE ARRANGEMENT, ETC., ON THE S.V. ENGINE

The exploded view shown applies to a 1952–8 S.V. engine. Earlier engines have a set-bolt fixing for the cylinder head instead of studs and nuts
(*By courtesy of* "*Motor Cycle,*" *London*)

piston down so that it is near the bottom of its stroke, and raise the cylinder barrel gently upwards and forwards. As the piston emerges, support it to prevent its skirt hitting the connecting-rod or the crankcase. For safety, cover up the crankcase mouth with a clean cloth.

98　　　　　　THE BOOK OF THE ARIEL

To Remove Cylinder Head (1954–60 Coil-ignition "Colts"). First turn off the petrol tap and disconnect the petrol pipe. Next remove the petrol tank as described on page 95, and also the sparking plug. Then proceed to remove the Amal carburettor after taking out the two flange securing-bolts. Unscrew the mixing-chamber cap ring (2, Fig. 12), pull the throttle

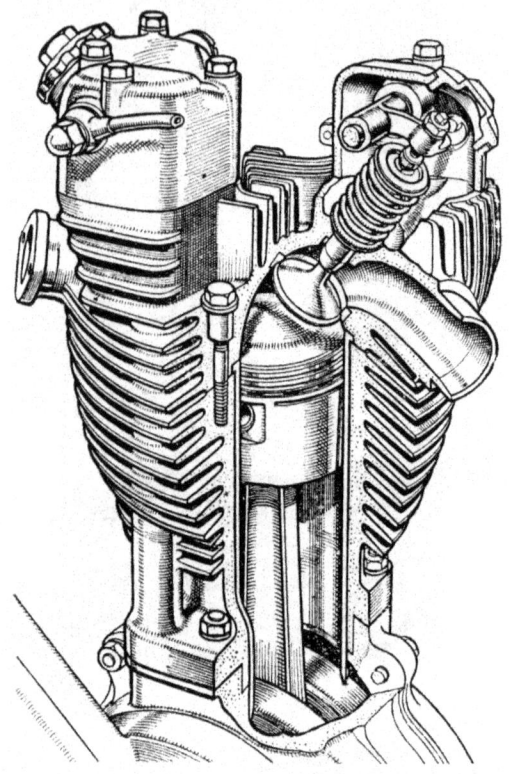

FIG. 53. CUT-AWAY VIEW OF CYLINDER HEAD AND BARREL ON TYPICAL O.H.V. ENGINE ("MAGDYNO" TYPE)

On some 1952–3 "Red Hunters" (Model VHA) the cylinder barrel is of aluminium alloy and has a detachable sleeve as shown

(*By courtesy of "Motor Cycle," London*)

valve right out, tie it up to the frame top-tube, and remove the complete instrument. Remove the exhaust pipe and silencer. The pipe is a push fit in the exhaust port, and the pipe and silencer can be readily removed as a unit after releasing the bolts securing the exhaust system to the frame.

Now remove the aluminium cover from the rocker-box after removing

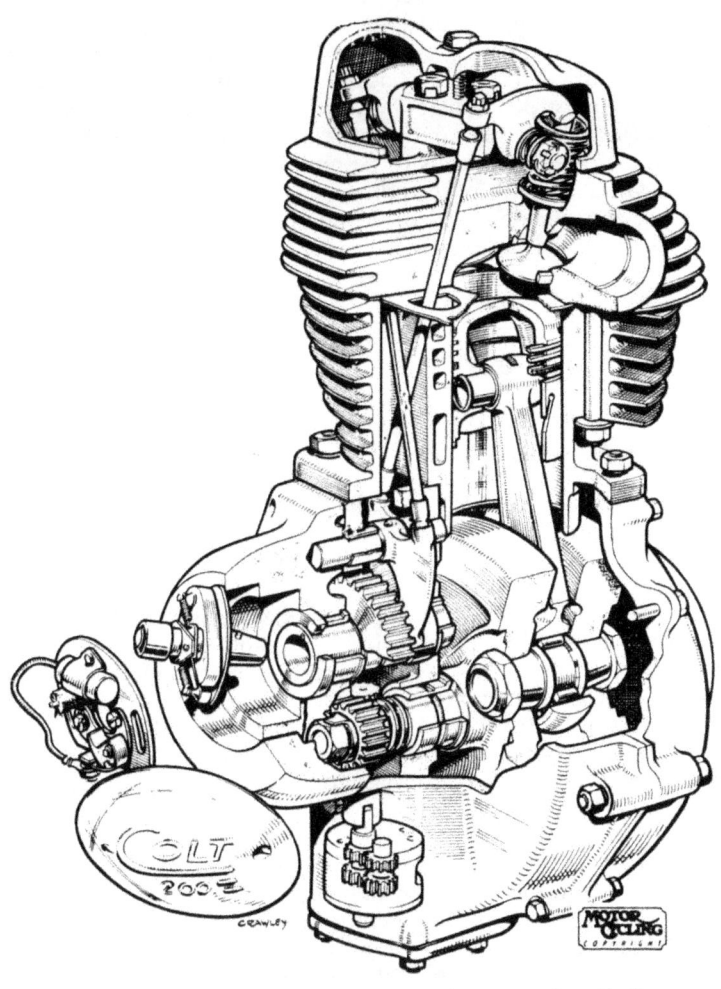

Fig. 54. Cut-away View of 200 c.c. O.H.V. "Colt" Engine

The contact-breaker unit and the automatic ignition advance mechanism are shown withdrawn from the 1954–60 power unit illustrated

(*By courtesy of "Motor Cycling"*)

its central securing bolt. Examine the gasket and look for evidence of oil-leakage. If such exists, the gasket should be scrapped and renewed.

Set the piston so that it is at top-dead-centre on the compression stroke so that both valves are fully closed and no pressure is imposed on any components of the rocker-box. Slacken the seven cylinder head securing-nuts in the reverse order to that shown in Fig. 63. These nuts are located between the fins and the sides of the barrel. Raise the cylinder head enough to enable the crossed push-rods to be removed from the overhead rocker ball-pins; withdraw both push-rods.

Now raise the cylinder head from the cylinder barrel and gently withdraw the head and its gasket, which should be bright all over and in sound

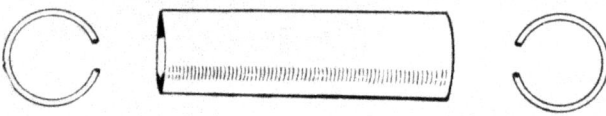

FIG. 55. THE GUDGEON-PIN AND CIRCLIPS
Circlips must always spring out firmly into the piston-boss grooves

condition. Should the gasket have black stained patches, this indicates that there has been gas leakage, and a new gasket must be fitted on assembly.

To Remove Cylinder Barrel (1954-60 Coil-ignition "Colts"). After removing the rocker-box cover, push-rods, and cylinder head, remove evenly the nuts securing the cylinder barrel to the crankcase, position the piston so that it is at the bottom of its stroke, and withdraw the cylinder barrel upwards and forwards. When it emerges from the piston, support the latter to prevent its hitting the crankcase or connecting-rod, and do not omit to cover the crankcase mouth with a clean cloth for obvious safety reasons.

Piston Removal. The piston (whose removal is seldom necessary) is of aluminium alloy with two compression rings and one slotted scraper ring (Fig. 56.) It is held to the small-end of the connecting-rod by a fully-floating gudgeon-pin secured to the piston by two circlips. These circlips fit snugly into grooves machined at both outer ends of the gudgeon-pin holes in the piston. The gudgeon-pin is a free fit in the small-end bush, but with the *engine cold* is a *tight fit* on most "Magdyno" models, and all 200 c.c. O.H.V. "Colts."

To remove the gudgeon-pin without risking damaging the piston, first *warm the piston* by laying an electric iron on its crown, or by wrapping round the piston a rag immersed in boiling water and wrung out. Then press out the gudgeon-pin after removing the circlips. Note that it is good policy to renew all circlips after removal. To remove the circlips, use a

GENERAL MAINTENANCE

small screwdriver or the tang end of a ground file, or a similar pointed instrument. Where a piston has seen considerable service, and on engines (excluding "Colt" engines) where the gudgeon-pin is an easy fit with the piston warm, it may be possible to push out the pin by hand. If this is not practicable, press out the gudgeon-pin with a gudgeon-pin extractor tool such as the Terry, or tap it out (supporting the piston on the opposite side) with a light hammer and soft-nosed punch.

It is important to scratch a slight nick on one end of the gudgeon-pin to enable the pin to be replaced in the same position.

Marking the Piston. Where the piston has a slot in its skirt at the *front* end, this can be used to ensure replacement in the correct position. Where no slot is provided, scratch an "F" mark on the *inside* of the piston to indicate which is the front. A piston can easily be distorted or cracked, as it is somewhat brittle. Therefore always handle it with the utmost care.

Piston Ring Inspection and Removal. The piston rings are responsible for maintaining good compression. Therefore they must be full of spring, free in their grooves, and set with their slots opposite to each other (i.e. at 120° on the three-ring piston which is fitted on all Ariel engines). If all three rings are bright all the way round, they are obviously being polished against the cylinder walls, and are perfect, and should be left alone. If, on the other hand, they are discoloured (brown marks) at some points, they are not in proper contact with the walls of the cylinder, causing gas to blow past them. Perhaps they are stuck in their grooves with burnt oil, and will function properly if the grooves are cleaned. If the rings are scored, or have lost their tension, or are vertically loose in their grooves, or have brown patches, the rings must be renewed.

Piston rings are of cast-iron and, being of very small section, must be handled very, very carefully. If not, they will certainly be broken. A scraper ring is particularly vulnerable: rings cannot safely be opened out wider than will allow them to slip over the crown of the piston. Therefore, to put them on or remove them it is advisable to insert small strips of sheet-metal, about ¾ in. wide by 2 in. long, which are placed in the manner shown by Fig. 56. Be most careful to note the order in which the rings are removed to ensure correct replacement. When fitting piston rings, thoroughly clean the grooves into which they fit, as any deposit left at the back of new rings forces them out and makes them too tight a fit. Paraffin usually loosens stuck piston rings.

When renewing piston rings, always fit rings supplied by Ariel Motors, Ltd., or one of their approved dealers. Piston rings are made to extremely fine limits and on new engines have a side clearance of 0·003 in. in their grooves. Never attempt to fit oversize rings to compensate for wear unless an oversize piston and a rebore are necessary. Pistons 0·020 in. and 0·040 in. oversize, with similar oversize rings to suit, are available.

The gap for all new piston rings, tested in an unworn part (the top or bottom) of the bore, on Ariel engines should be 0·006 in.–0·008 in. (0·008 in. –0·012 in. on "Colts"). It is advisable when it is necessary to remove the piston to check the gaps of all three piston rings, using suitable feeler gauges. Renew any ring whose gap exceeds 0·025 in.–0·030 in. If new standard or oversize rings are fitted, check their gaps before fitting them to the piston. When checking the gaps, insert each piston ring into an unworn part of the cylinder bore and slide up the piston afterwards so that its crown contacts and squares up the ring.

Scrutinize the ends of each ring. If they are bright, the ring gap is too small; if, on the other hand, they are heavily coated with carbon, the gap is probably excessive. Should the gap of a ring be less than 0·006 in. (0·008 in. on "Colts") clamp the ring between two wooden blocks in a vice and file one of the diagonal ends slightly. If a new ring is found to be rather a tight fit in its groove, rub down one side of the ring on a sheet of carborundum paper laid flat on a piece of plate-glass. The slotted scraper ring (see Fig. 56) fitted to Ariel pistons can be fitted either way up. All three rings should be assembled, using the safe method shown in Fig. 56.

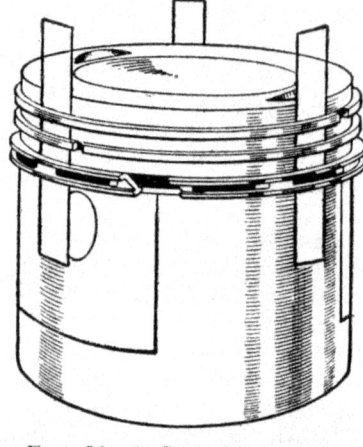

FIG. 56. A SAFE METHOD OF REMOVING PISTON RINGS

The method (see text) can also be used for fitting rings. Note the slotted scraper ring below the two compression rings. The top ring is chromium-plated and must not be interchanged with the second ring

A final word of good advice: if engine compression is good and the piston is doing its job well, leave the piston rings alone.

Removing Carbon from Cylinder Head. Carbon forms less readily on smooth surfaces; therefore always decarbonize thoroughly. Remove all carbon deposits from the cylinder head with a proprietary scraper, a blunt knife, or a blunt screwdriver. Be careful not to scratch deeply the combustion chamber, especially where the engine has a light-alloy head. The author finds that a small electrical screwdriver is excellent for decarbonizing the curved walls of the combustion chamber. To avoid damaging the valve seats in the head, always first insert the valves in their guides.

Remove *all* traces of carbon from the interior surfaces and do not forget the sparking plug hole and the exhaust port(s). If a curved rifler is used to clean up the port channels, be particularly careful not to allow the pointed end of the rifler to scratch the valve seats. Carbon deposits having

GENERAL MAINTENANCE

been removed, it is permissible, though not really necessary, to polish a *cast-iron* type head with fine emery cloth, but do this *before* removing the valves, and afterwards clean all abrasive particles away with paraffin. Also scrape all carbon deposits from the heads of the valves.

Where an aluminium-alloy head is concerned, never use emery cloth or any other abrasive to clean the combustion chamber, and in no circumstances attempt to remove carbon by immersing the head in a hot caustic-soda or potash solution. Results will be disastrous.

Decarbonizing the Piston. With the comparatively soft aluminium-alloy piston, be careful when removing the carbon. *Do not use emery cloth,*

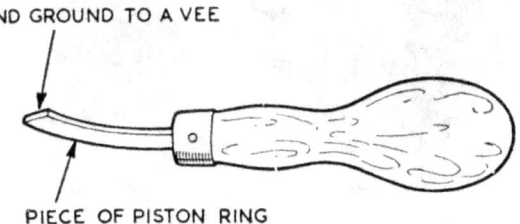

FIG. 57. A USEFUL TOOL FOR CLEANING PISTON-RING GROOVES

but only a blunt knife, a proprietary scraper, or a blunt screwdriver. Do not attempt to remove carbon from the piston skirt or the lands between the rings. A little carbon is sometimes deposited on the inside of the piston, and this should be carefully scraped off if the piston is removed. Where a screwdriver is used, be careful not to allow the screwdriver shank to bump against the piston skirt.

Inspect the piston-ring grooves for carbon deposits; scrape any deposits off, using a proprietary scraper or a home-made tool such as that shown in Fig. 57. Do not forget to scrape carbon off the backs of the rings. Having decarbonized the piston and rings, wash them thoroughly in clean paraffin. Refit the rings by slipping them over the piston, using preferably the method shown in Fig. 56.

Carbon on Cylinder Barrel. Some riders remove the thin ring of carbon which forms round the top of the cylinder bore above the piston T.D.C. position. This is strongly deprecated because the carbon forms a most efficient oil seal, thereby reducing oil consumption and postponing the formation of carbon deposits in the cylinder head.

Removing Valves (All S.V. Models). Place the cylinder (if there has been occasion to remove it) on its side, valve-spring chamber upwards, and remove the valves, using a valve-spring compressor, which may be obtained from most accessory dealers (*see* page 77) or Ariel stockists. The forked end is placed under the valve collar and the point of the screw in the small centre-hole in the valve head. Screw up, compressing the spring, and then remove the split collet. Unscrew the compressor and remove the valve, valve spring, and collars. Both valves are dealt with in this manner. Fig. 58 shows a Model VB cylinder removed, with the inlet valve withdrawn and the exhaust-valve spring being compressed.

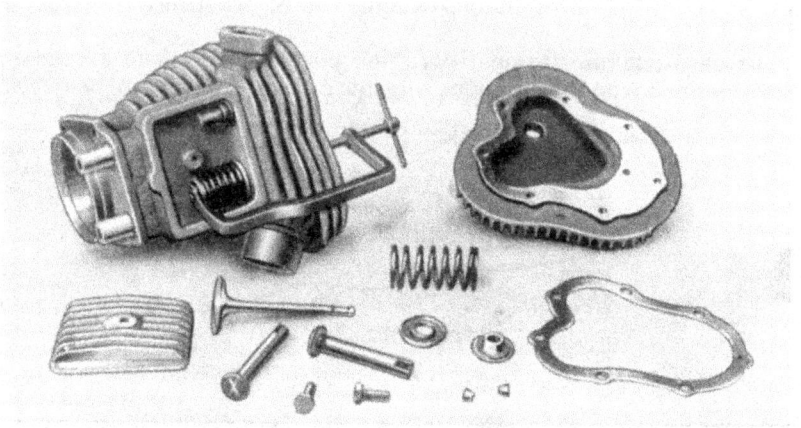

FIG. 58. USING VALVE-SPRING COMPRESSOR ON S.V. ENGINE TO REMOVE VALVE

On Model VB it is, of course, *not* necessary to remove the cylinder barrel. The cylinder head, the cylinder barrel and various valve components are shown removed for general illustration purposes

If it is intended to grind-in the valves without removing the cylinder barrel, block up the bore with a rag, rotate the engine until both valves are closed, slack off the tappets, and proceed as just described. After removing the valves be careful to see that they are not subsequently interchanged. The inlet valve is stamped "IN" while the exhaust valve is stamped "EX." Note their difference in colour.

Removing Valves (All O.H.V.). Owing to different cylinder-head design, the exact type of valve-spring compressor shown in Fig. 58 is not suitable, but a screw-type compressor specially designed for the purpose (*see* Fig. 59) is obtainable for a modest sum from any Ariel stockist or most accessory dealers. The method of using this tool is precisely the same as in the case of the S.V. models. Remove the valve-stem end-caps (where fitted). Place the forked end on the valve-spring collar and the pointed end of the screw in the centre of the valve head and screw up until the valve spring is sufficiently compressed to allow the split collet to be removed. If stuck,

GENERAL MAINTENANCE 105

gently tap the forked end of the valve-spring compressor. The valve, valve springs, and collars can now be removed. Deal with each valve similarly. Fig. 59 shows, in addition to the valve-spring compressor being used on the inlet valve, details of the rocker-boxes.

As on the other engines, avoid interchanging the valves after removal. The inlet and exhaust valves are stamped "IN" and "EX" respectively.

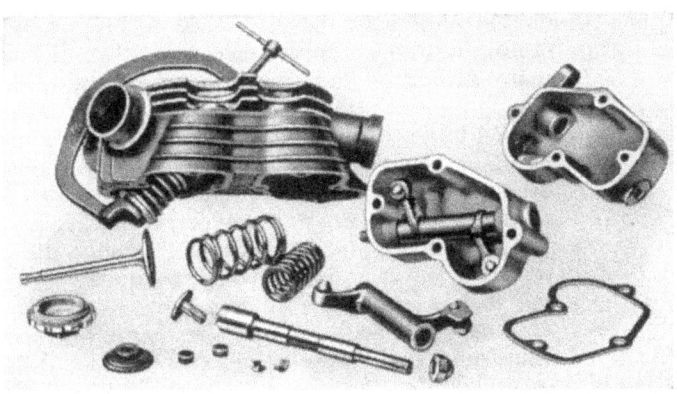

FIG. 59. USING VALVE SPRING COMPRESSOR ON O.H.V. ENGINE ("MAGDYNO" MODEL) TO REMOVE VALVE

For illustration purposes the contents of one rocker-box are shown removed. A similar type of valve spring compressor is suitable for removing the valves on O.H.V. "Colt" engines which have a single non-detachable rocker-box (*see* Fig. 54)

Grinding-in the Valves. Should the valve faces or seats show signs of pitting, the valves will have to be ground-in. Valves of the side-by-side type have, of course, to be *pressed down* on their seatings when using a screwdriver, while those of the overhead type have to be *pulled up* against their seatings.

Deal with each valve in the following manner. Clean both the valve face and its seat in the cylinder head. Smear a thin film of fine grinding paste (coarse at first if dealing with a valve and seat in poor condition) with a piece of rag or the finger tip on the valve face; replace the valve in its guide minus the valve spring.

It will facilitate grinding-in the valves on the S.V. engines if a small compression spring is inserted under the valve head. This avoids the nuisance of having to lift the valve repeatedly by hand to change it to a new position. Also put the piston near bottom-dead-centre and block up the cylinder bore with a clean rag. Slacken off both tappets.

On O.H.V. engines the valve-grinding tool shown in Fig. 60 is recommended. When using this tool it is advisable to moisten the suction pad. Only a light pressure on the tool is required and care must be taken not to rock the valve, particularly if the valve guide is somewhat worn. Rotate the valve about *a third of a turn* in one direction and then an equal amount in the opposite direction, pausing every few oscillations to raise the valve from its seat and turn it one-third to a quarter of a revolution. Cease grinding-in when no "cut" can be felt (and the valve begins to "sing") and put some more paste on the bevelled edge of the valve face if, after cleaning the valve in paraffin, some pitting is still visible.

Continue grinding-in until both the valve face and seat have a matt metallic surface uniformly over an appreciable depth (line contact is not really sufficient) and there are no pit marks left after wiping the paste off. Excessive grinding-in after a good seating has been effected eventually leads to the valves becoming "pocketed," which causes a considerable decline in power output. Badly-pitted valves or seats require to be refaced by a competent mechanic.

After grinding-in the inlet and exhaust valves, wipe both the valves and their seats thoroughly clean with a rag soaked in paraffin or petrol to ensure that there is absolutely no trace of any abrasive left. Examine the valve guides for wear and renew if much play exists, otherwise slow-running will become difficult. Often a valve stem wears more than its guide does, and a distinct shoulder is felt near the neck of the valve. In this case fitting a new valve (which must be ground-in) will probably remedy slackness without fitting a new valve guide.

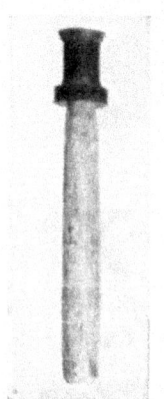

FIG. 60. VALVE-GRINDING TOOL (O.H.V.)

Checking Condition of Valve Springs. After completing a big mileage the valve springs may weaken through continuous heat and movement. This applies particularly to the exhaust-valve spring. The best time to check the condition of the valve springs is when decarbonizing, as this avoids any unnecessary dismantling. To check the condition of the springs, *compare them for length*. If one spring is shorter than the other one, renew the *shorter* spring immediately.

Refitting the Valves. After grinding-in the valves you should reassemble them in the correct positions (*see* page 104) in the cylinder head.

Do not forget to replace the hardened valve-stem end-caps (where fitted), i.e., 500 c.c. engines. Before replacing the valve springs, check that they have not lost their tension. Loss of tension, due mainly to heat, sometimes occurs after several thousand miles, and the free length of the valve springs is reduced. This necessitates renewal and where such renewal is, or soon will be, required, it is obviously wise to effect valve-spring renewal during decarbonizing procedure.

Smear the valve stems with oil and replace them in their guides. Then refit the valve springs and the inner and outer collars, being careful not to mix up the inlet and exhaust components. Next compress each valve spring and refit the split collet, making certain that it "beds down" properly. The application of a little grease to the groove on the valve stem enables the split collet to stick on the valve stem until the duplex spring is released, and thereby facilitates reassembly. To ensure the split collet bedding down, hold a box spanner over the outer collar and tap sharply. Do not forget to replace the valve-stem end-caps (where provided).

After Reassembly. It is an excellent plan to test the valve seats by pouring some petrol into the ports and watching for leakage past the valves. Petrol should not creep past the valves until after a considerable time has elapsed. If it does, then this is sure proof that the valves have not been sufficiently ground-in and the remedy is (horrible thought!) to remove and continue grinding-in. *The ultimate test of good valve seating is engine compression.*

Replacing the Piston. Fit a *new* circlip into one of the piston-boss annular grooves, using a small pair of snipe-nose pliers; see that the circlip beds down snugly and is fully expanded (a loose circlip can ruin the bore). If the gudgeon-pin is not a push fit in the piston bosses (it rarely is), warm up the piston in a bowl of boiling water before fitting it to the small-end of the connecting-rod.

With the crankcase mouth protected by a cloth and the piston held in its normal position, start the gudgeon-pin into the piston-boss hole opposite to where the circlip has been fitted. Before fitting the gudgeon-pin, make sure that it is the correct way round (*see* page 101) and smear it liberally with some clean engine oil. Then tap in the pin, holding the piston firmly on the opposite side and using a soft-nose hammer or small mallet. If the gudgeon-pin is a tight fit, press the pin in, using a proprietary tool such as the Terry. As soon as the gudgeon-pin contacts the circlip already fitted, fit a *new* circlip on the other side.

To Replace the Cylinder Barrel (All S.V.). The following procedure is recommended—

1. Check that the joint faces of the cylinder barrel and the crankcase are scrupulously clean and fit a new cylinder-base paper washer to the crankcase face, after smearing it lightly with some jointing compound. Make absolutely sure that the small hole in the base washer registers exactly with the oil-drain hole from the base of the valve chest.

2. Turn the engine over slowly so that the piston is just past B.D.C.

3. Smear the piston (especially the rings) and the bore of the cylinder barrel with some clean engine oil, and space the ring gaps so that they are at 120 degrees to each other. With a split-skirt piston, see that no gap is in the immediate vicinity of the split in the skirt.

4. Hold the cylinder barrel vertically over the crankcase studs and piston with one hand, and with the other offer up the piston to the barrel mouth. If difficulty is experienced in holding the piston and barrel steady, it is best to obtain assistance or to tie up the barrel to the frame top-tube with some stout string. Keep the barrel and piston absolutely square to each other and squeeze the rings by hand or with a proprietary metal strap (without disturbing the ring-gap position) as the piston slowly enters the bore. If a ring sticks, use no force, or the ring will break.

5. When the cylinder barrel has bedded right down on the base washer, turn the engine over slowly to verify that the piston is quite free.

6. Fit and tighten the four nuts securing the cylinder base to the crankcase evenly (*a half-turn at a time*) and in a diagonal order, after first checking that both tappets are right down*.

7. Reconnect the exhaust-valve lifter control-cable to the small lever shown in Fig. 61.

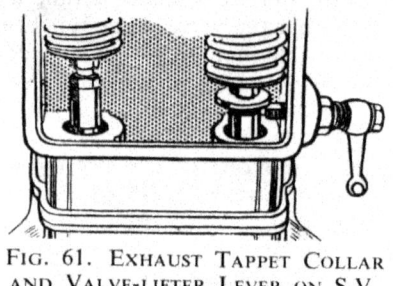

FIG. 61. EXHAUST TAPPET COLLAR AND VALVE-LIFTER LEVER ON S.V. ENGINE

To Replace Cylinder Barrel (All O.H.V.). On "Magdyno" models and on the coil-ignition "Colt" models, replace the cylinder barrel as previously described for the S.V. engines, but disregard: (*a*) the reference (paragraph 1) about the small hole in the cylinder-base washer registering with the oil-drain hole from the base of the valve chest; (*b*) all reference (paragraph 7) to the exhaust-valve lifter control cable.

Final Assembly (1939–58 S.V.). On the Model VB Ariel final assembly is very straightforward. First check that the joint faces of the cylinder barrel and cylinder head are absolutely clean, and position the copper-asbestos gasket (*see* Fig. 52) which must also be clean and undamaged. Replace the seven or nine set-bolts (*see* page 96), or the nine hexagon nuts and plain washers used for securing most of the light-alloy cylinder heads.

Screw down the set-bolts or nuts until the heads of the set-bolts, or the nuts, are in finger-tight contact with the cylinder head. Then with the appropriate spanner give one set-bolt or nut a *one-eighth turn*. Repeat this tightening on the next but one set-bolt or nut, proceeding so to the last one. Work right round the head in this manner until all the set-bolts or nuts are firmly tightened. This method of tightening ensures an even

* Should the tappets have been previously dismantled for any reason, make sure that the lock-nut with the large collar is fitted to the *exhaust* tappet (*see* Fig. 61). The exhaust-valve lifter collar comes above the nut.

pressure on the joint face, and eliminates the possibility of any subsequent gas leakage.

Replace the sparking plug and its copper washer, attach the H.T. lead to the plug; fit the valve-chest cover and its washer, and the Amal carburettor and exhaust system (if previously removed). Assembly is now completed. Start the engine and run gently until it is warmed up. Then check the tappet clearances (*see* page 88), and check the cylinder barrel and cylinder head nuts (or set-bolts) for tightness. Give a final tightening with the engine still hot after running about 30 miles.

Final Assembly (1939–60 O.H.V. "Magdyno" Models). It is assumed that the cylinder barrel is in position, or has been replaced if removed during decarbonizing. Turn the engine over so that the piston is at top-dead-centre (on the compression stroke), with neither cam lever on the lift (the fully-closed valve position). Make sure that all parts removed are absolutely clean, and that no grinding paste has been left anywhere. Check that the joint faces of the cylinder head and cylinder barrel are absolutely smooth and clean. No joint washer is required but on all the engines it is desirable to smear a little jointing compound on the joint face of the cylinder head before replacing the head.

On all 1939–53 engines and 1954 350 c.c. engines, fit new rubber washers to the push-rod covers to prevent oil leakage. Locate these covers round the spigot below the head and lower the head and cover assembly into position. On all 1956–60 engines the push-rods are enclosed by cast-in channels on the cylinder barrel. In this case before lowering the head, fit new rubber washers to the push-rod enclosing top channel.

Insert the four cylinder-head securing bolts, screw them in a few turns and make sure that the push-rod covers (where fitted) are correctly located at each end and that the head correctly fits the spigot of the cylinder barrel. Screw down the bolts finger-tight and then with a spanner put extra tension on the two bolts near the push-rod tubes or channels (1956–8) until the rubber washers have been squeezed down sufficiently to allow the head to make contact with the barrel all round the joint face.

Now give one bolt a *one-eighth turn* and repeat on the bolt diagonally opposite. Do the same on the two remaining bolts. Return to the first bolt, give it another one-eighth turn, repeat on the opposite bolt and then on the other two, and so on, working round the head from one bolt to another until all are perfectly tight. This will ensure a good gas-tight joint. Insert the two push-rods, and do not interchange them.

See that the rocker-box joint faces are clean, both on the head and on each box, and examine the joint washers. If these are damaged fit new ones, or an oil-tight joint will not be obtained. Lay the washers in position on the head and take one of the boxes and the *long* bolt which passes through the push-rod end of the box. Slip this bolt through the box and then put the box in position, but hold it about half an inch above the head.

Start the bolt by two or three threads and then, using the bolt as a guide, slide the box down on to the joint face. If this is done carefully the ball end on the rocker will drop into the push-rod cup; check this by testing the rocker for up and down play through the adjustment cover hole, whilst holding the box down firmly with the hand. When the rocker and push-rod have engaged, insert the three short bolts and carefully tighten

FIG. 62. THE ENGINE ON A TYPICAL O.H.V. "MAGDYNO" MODEL COMPLETELY ASSEMBLED AFTER DECARBONIZING

The engine shown is a 350 c.c. "Red Hunter" (Model NH), with aluminium-alloy cylinder head having valve-seat inserts. Neatness of the air-cleaner arrangement, and the accessibility of the Burman four-speed gearbox are two features of an excellent layout

all four, pulling down each bolt a little at a time as was done for the cylinder head. Now fit the other rocker-box in a similar manner.

Replace the carburettor, sparking plug exhaust system, etc., and replace the petrol tank as described on page 95.

Final Assembly (1954–60 O.H.V. Coil-ignition "Colts"). Check that the cylinder head gasket is sound, with no evidence of "blowing." Then replace and fit the cylinder head loosely in position. Fit the push-rods down their appropriate apertures before tightening the cylinder head nuts. As may be seen in Fig. 54, the push-rods must be fitted so that the inlet and

GENERAL MAINTENANCE

exhaust rods cross. First fit the exhaust push-rod so that its plain end fits into the cup formed on the cam rocker (bottom left), and the cupped end fits over the ball end of the exhaust-rocker screw (top right). Now bolt the cylinder head firmly down, using the order shown in Fig. 63.

Check the valve clearances (page 91) before replacing the rocker-box cover and gasket (which must be undamaged) and make whatever adjustment is necessary. After covering 250 miles, check the cylinder head securing-nuts for tightness. If tightening is required, check the valve clearances and, if necessary, effect an adjustment.

Replace the Amal carburettor, taking care not to damage the jet needle when inserting the throttle slide. See that the washer for the carburettor flange is sound, otherwise air leaks will cause poor starting. Replace the exhaust system and secure it firmly. Dismantle and clean the plug; replace it; fit the H.T. lead; and finally fit the petrol tank and fuel pipe. Wire-lock the two rear tank bolts.

IGNITION AND VALVE TIMING

The Ignition Timing. Some motor-cyclists imagine that by advancing the timing they will automatically obtain greater speed. The timing recommended by the engine manufacturers is the maximum advance permissible. A further advance in the timing submits the big-end bearing to undue stresses and spoils the flexibility of the engine; it is also likely to cause some spitting-back through the carburettor. Always employ the correct ignition timings which are given on page 113.

If for any reason a Lucas "Magdyno," or a Wipac contact-breaker unit and mounting plate ("Colts") are removed or the driving pinion is freed or extracted from its tapered shaft, it is necessary to retime the ignition. This should be done in accordance with the instructions which follow.

Timing the Ignition (All Lucas "Magdyno" Models). Before checking the ignition timing, or retiming the ignition, always clean the contacts (where necessary) and check that the gap between them, with the contacts fully open, is 0·012–0·015 in. (*see* pages 83–4). An incorrect gap affects the timing to some extent. Also check the "Magdyno" chain tension (*see* page 114).

To retime, first remove the sparking plug and take off the aluminium chain-case cover from the engine. Then without removing the chain undo the nut securing the sprocket to the armature shaft. The sprocket may then be released from the shaft taper. If necessary, use an Ariel extractor (obtainable from Ariel stockists), but be careful not to impose any strain on the armature.

Turn the engine slowly *forward* until the piston is at the top of the compression stroke, with both valves fully closed. Next move the ignition lever on the handlebars to the fully advanced position (*see* page 7); keep it in this position until retiming is completed. See that the stop-screw in

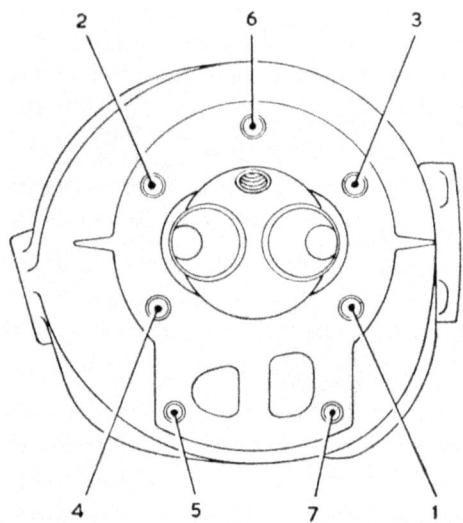

FIG. 63. CORRECT ORDER OF TIGHTENING CYLINDER-HEAD NUTS ON 200 C.C. O.H.V. "COLT" ENGINE

FIG. 64. ASSEMBLED POWER UNIT ON A COIL-IGNITION O.H.V. "COLT" MODEL

The neat enclosure of all parts is very noticeable. The circular cover on the engine, held by two screws, encloses the contact-breaker and automatic ignition-advance mechanism

the magneto cam-plate is in the end of the slot and that the plate is not sticking. If the control lever is slack, tighten the lever nut before proceeding further.

Turn the engine slowly *backwards* (by means of the rear wheel with third or top gear engaged) until the piston has descended a distance below T.D.C. corresponding exactly to the maximum ignition-advance (*see below*). To find true T.D.C., where the cylinder head has *not* been removed, use a simply-made T.D.C. indicator. Screw the body of an old sparking plug into the plug hole. Then insert a piece of thick wire, or thin rod, bent over at one end for safety, through the hole in the centre of the plug body. Then mark with some red adhesive plastic, or scratch with a thin file a nick on the wire immediately above the top of the hole, when slightly rocking the crank produces no piston movement.

Make another mark $\frac{1}{2}$ in. (or whatever is the correct ignition advance) above the first mark, and when turning the engine backwards to obtain the correct piston position for timing, allow the second mark to occupy the position of the first (T.D.C.) mark. Should the cylinder head be removed for decarbonizing the best method is to lay a straight edge across the top of the barrel and take vertical measurement with a steel rule. This gives a very precise timing.

Some owners prefer to retime the ignition by taking degree measurements of crankshaft rotation, using a degree disc, but this is quite unnecessary for normal purposes.

Having obtained the correct position of the piston when the spark should occur with the ignition lever fully advanced, turn the magneto shaft by hand (in its normal direction of rotation) so that the contacts of the contact-breaker are just beginning to open; the best method of determining the point at which the contacts "break" is to insert a small slip of thin cellophane or tissue-paper between the contacts and gently pull on this as the contact-breaker cam is slowly turned; immediately the slip is freed, stop moving the magneto shaft to which the cam is fitted. Replace the "Magdyno" driving sprocket on the tapered end of the magneto shaft and, being careful not to turn the engine, tap it home lightly, using a box spanner and light hammer to direct even pressure on the sprocket boss. Lock the sprocket to the shaft by fitting and tightening the lock-nut. When doing this, it is advisable to engage a gear and lock the rear wheel so as to prevent the engine turning. Before replacing the timing-case cover and washer, it is advisable to recheck the ignition timing.

Correct Ignition Timings (All "Magdyno" Models). On the S.V. engines (Model VB) the ignition timing is correct when the piston is $\frac{5}{16}$ in. (1939–49), $\frac{1}{4}$ in. (1950–3), or $\frac{11}{32}$ in. (1954–8) before T.D.C. with the ignition lever *fully advanced.*

On 1939–50 O.H.V. engines (not "Red Hunters" or engines with "Red Hunter" cam assembly) the correct ignition advance is $\frac{3}{8}$ in. before T.D.C.

with the ignition lever *fully advanced*. On certain 1946–50 O.H.V. engines (VG and NG, with engine numbers later than CR2001 and BK2753 respectively) the correct ignition timing is ⅜ in. and ½ in. before T.D.C. respectively, with the ignition lever *fully advanced*.

On all 1939–60 "Red Hunter" engines (350 c.c. and 500 c.c.) the correct ignition advance for normal touring (with standard low-compression plate fitted) is ½ in. before T.D.C., with the ignition lever *fully advanced*. For fast driving (with high-compression plate fitted) the correct ignition timing is ⅝ in. before T.D.C., with the ignition lever *fully advanced*.

Timing the Ignition (1954–60 O.H.V. "Colts"). In the event of it becoming necessary for any reason to remove the complete Wipac contact-breaker assembly and mounting plate, the ignition must be re-timed during assembly.

Referring to Fig. 45, the mounting plate is secured in position by two screws (*C*) and (*D*). The two slots in the mounting plate receive screws (*C*) and (*D*) and it can readily be observed that a limited clockwise or anti-clockwise movement of the mounting plate can be obtained before the screws are tightened down.

To time the ignition correctly, first remove the sparking plug to enable the engine to be turned over slowly by hand. Position the piston at T.D.C. as described on page 111 for the "Magdyno" models, and then turn the engine gently backwards until the piston is found to be exactly 1/16 in. before top-dead-centre (*see* page 113).

With the piston correctly positioned, and the contact-breaker (*see* Fig. 54) properly located, but with the two securing screws (*C*) and (*D*) slack, turn the mounting plate clockwise or anti-clockwise as required until the contact points (Fig. 45) are just beginning to open, with the ignition control *fully retarded*. The ignition timing is in the fully retarded position when the engine is not running, the design of the automatic ignition advance-and-retard mechanism making any manual movement quite unnecessary.

"Magdyno" Chain Tension (S.V. and O.H.V. Engines). Being completely enclosed, automatically lubricated from the engine, and moving at only half engine speed, the chain wears very slowly. Before checking the ignition timing, however, and after a very considerable mileage, it is advisable to check that the chain tension is correct. With the chain in its tightest position there should be about ⅜ in. up-and-down movement in the centre of the chain.

To adjust the chain tension, with the chain-case cover removed, loosen the two set-bolts which secure the "Magdyno" to its mounting platform and then slide the instrument backwards or forwards as required until the chain tension is found to be correct. Afterwards carefully re-tighten the two set-bolts and make sure that the "Magdyno" is held close up to the back of the chain-case cover, otherwise oil leakage may occur because of the oil-sealing washer becoming displaced.

Should it become necessary to renew the oil-sealing rubber washer or to remove the "Magdyno" for any reason, note that the following assembly sequence is essential: (1) fit the small oil-sealing washer on the armature shaft, so that it abuts the back end-plate of the "Magdyno"; (2) fit the metal retaining washer or plate; (3) fit the large oil-sealing rubber washer

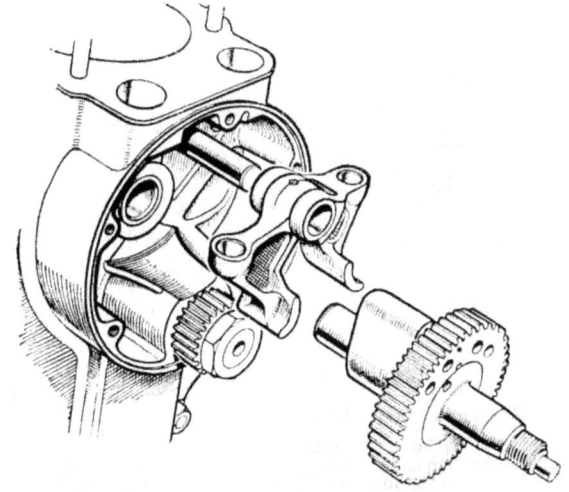

Fig. 65. Showing the Single Camwheel Timing Gear (S.V. and O.H.V.)

To ensure correct replacement of the Ariel camwheel there is a single small dot-mark (located between two pairs of holes on the camwheel face) close to one tooth-space on the camwheel and this dot mark must *always* register with a similar dot-mark near a tooth, on the engine pinion. The valve timing is then absolutely correct

Do not Interfere with Valve Timing. Whilst correct ignition timing is, as already mentioned, very important, correct valve timing is still more important. The exact moment when a valve opens and closes vitally affects engine performance and even an alteration in valve timing to the extent of one tooth only will produce a pronounced effect. Ariel engine designers know their job and it is, to say the least, a foolish and ignorant rider who would seek improved performance by "messing about" with the valve timing. To ensure correct replacement of the timing gear after a general overhaul, the manufacturers have adopted a system of marking the meshing timing gears on the S.V. and O.H.V. engines (*see* Fig. 65).

Dismantling Timing Gear (S.V. and O.H.V. "Magdyno" Models). To dismantle the timing gear first undo the seven set-screws which secure the

"Magdyno" chain-case cover and remove the cover. The complete oil pump can now be removed by detaching the two cheese-headed fixing screws holding the pump body (Fig. 28).* Next remove the two "Magdyno" drive sprockets with the Ariel sprocket extractor, after first removing the armature and camshaft nuts. As a precaution against damaging the camshaft eccentric (which operates the pump) the small cupped-adaptor (supplied with the extractor) should be slipped over it before attempting to remove the camshaft sprocket. After removing the two

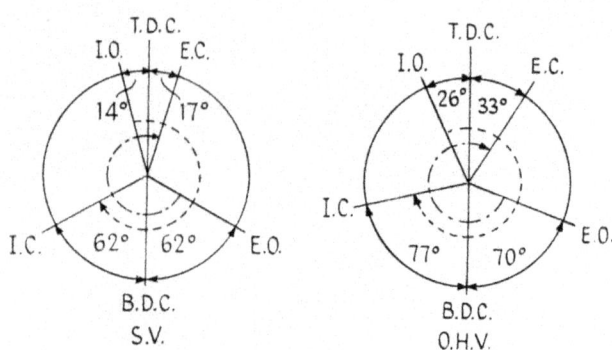

FIG. 66. 1951–8 VALVE TIMING DIAGRAMS FOR (LEFT) S.V. ENGINES AND (RIGHT) O.H.V. ENGINES ON "MAGDYNO" MODELS

During a valve-timing check, the tappet clearance on S.V. and O.H.V. engines (except "Red Hunters") must be 0·010 in. On the "Red Hunter" engines a temporary valve-clearance of 0·023 in.–0·025 in. is required

sprockets proceed to remove the delivery and return oil pipes and also the small pipe leading to the overhead rockers. Disconnect these at the connexions so that the unions remain in the timing cover.

Now proceed to slack off the set-bolt holding the "Magdyno" platform and remove the five set-screws securing the timing-case cover. Withdraw the cover and while doing so press against the end of the camshaft spindle to prevent it being pulled out of its bush and the timing upset. If it is desired to examine the cams, the camwheel can be pulled out and also the cam levers. It is a simple matter to reset the valve timing when reassembling.

Do not interfere with the small timing pinion on the mainshaft as the removal of this pinion is rarely necessary. It is keyed to the mainshaft and the lock-nut has a left-hand thread. The key ensures that the pinion is always refitted in exactly the same position on the shaft. To reset the valve timing after removing the camwheel, rotate the engine until the piston is on top-dead-centre, hold the camwheel, lift the cam levers and

* *See also* notes on page 55 concerning additional ball valves on 1957–9 "Magdyno" models.

insert the camwheel so that the timing dot marked on it coincides with a similar dot punched on the engine pinion (*see* Fig. 65). The valve timing will then be correct. When fitting the cam levers, first assemble them together by placing the plain or single end of the inlet lever into the forked or double end of the exhaust lever. Then place the assembly on the cam-lever spindle with the forked exhaust lever on the right-hand side position in the timing case. Note that on certain series of engines a thin steel shim is used to centralize the cam levers by placing it on the lever spindle either at the front or back of the lever assembly. After refitting the sprockets and tightening up the securing nuts firmly, see that the "Magdyno" driving chain is properly retensioned (*see* page 114). Before securing the armature sprocket, however, the magneto must be re-timed as described on page 111. Be careful to replace all joint washers and if any of them are damaged they must be renewed, or oil leakage may occur. When replacing the timing-case cover see that the paper washer is replaced and also be sure that there is an *additional paper washer* 0·005 in. thick at the joint connexion to the sump. Do up all nuts, screws, etc., thoroughly tight and do not forget the set-bolt which supports the "Magdyno" platform.

Dismantling Timing Gear (1954–60 O.H.V. "Colt" Engines). It is quite unnecessary to disturb the timing gear on a coil-ignition Ariel "Colt" except when undertaking a general overhaul. In this case the following is the correct procedure.

Remove the Ariel "Colt" name-plate or contact-breaker cover (*see* Fig. 64) after unscrewing the two securing screws. Disconnect the cable lead from the contact-breaker to the coil; there is one snap-connector. Now remove the two screws shown at (C) and (D) in Fig. 45. This will free the mounting plate. Next remove the long central hexagon-headed bolt which secures the automatic ignition advance-and-retard unit and its driving sleeve (*see* Fig. 54). The unit is located on a keyed tapered shaft and its removal involves using an improvised extractor such as a $3\frac{1}{2}$ in. long and $\frac{3}{16}$ in. diameter rod. Screw into the thread provided a $\frac{5}{16}$ in. B.S.C. 26 T.P.I. bolt, approximately $\frac{5}{8}$ in. long, and force the ignition advance-and-retard unit off its taper.

The camwheel can now be withdrawn and this necessitates the subsequent re-timing of the valves, and, of course, re-timing the ignition (*see* page 114) after replacing the camwheel, the ignition advance-and-retard unit, and the contact-breaker.

As regards the valve timing, one tooth-space of the camwheel, and one tooth of the crankshaft pinion are each etched with a dash mark as shown in Fig. 67. To ensure that the valve timing is correct, it is only necessary to position the piston at T.D.C. on the compression stroke (both valves closed) and then to engage the cam wheel with the crankshaft pinion so that the dash marks register with each other at every second crankshaft revolution.

On the "Colt" engine the inlet valve opens 25 degrees before T.D.C. and closes 70 degrees after B.D.C. The exhaust valve opens 70 degrees before B.D.C. and closes 25 degrees after T.D.C. If the timing-case cover is removed it is advisable to fit new washers on both sides to prevent any risk of oil leakage.

ENGINE STRIP AND ASSEMBLY HINTS

Assembling Oil Pump (S.V. and O.H.V. "Magdyno" Models). Be careful to place the joint washer correctly in position and tighten up the

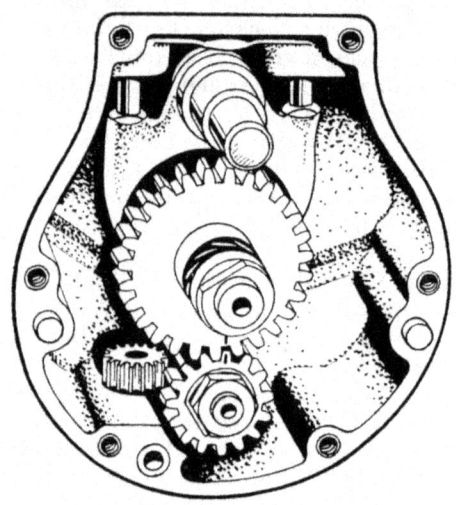

Fig. 67. Showing Valve Timing Marks on O.H.V. "Colt" Engine

set-screws securely. If the washer is damaged, fit a new one. It is of the greatest importance that a good joint is made between the pump face and the cover. Sometimes it is beneficial to fit an extra washer to ensure an oil-tight joint. The author does not advise removal of the pump unnecessarily. When replacing the duralumin block (Fig. 28) make sure that the chamfered end of the hole which engages the camshaft eccentric faces *inwards*.

Dismantling O.H.V. Rocker-boxes ("Magdyno" Models). If it is required to dismantle the rockers, first remove each rocker-box (*see* page 96); then remove the large flat-headed screw from the end of each rocker spindle next to the sparking plug. Now press or tap out the spindle towards the same end, thereby freeing the overhead rocker. Note the position of the double-coil distance-spring on the spindle end next to the flat-headed screw. When reassembling, see that the flat distance-washer is fitted on the spindle between the rocker and the rocker-box on the opposite right-hand side. This washer prevents the rocker rubbing the soft aluminium and also forms an abutment against which the spindle is pulled when the outer oil union retaining-nuts are screwed up. The flat-headed screw at the other end in conjunction with the fibre washer is nothing but an oil seal, and must be tightened *after* the oil-union nuts have been tightened.

Removing Overhead Rockers (O.H.V. "Colt" Engines). Should you for any reason wish to remove the overhead rockers from the rocker-box, withdraw the split-pins and unscrew the nuts holding the rockers in position (*see* Fig. 54). Note the exact location of all parts. It is important when replacing the components to fit the various washers in their original positions.

Connecting-rod Bearings. When there is occasion to remove the cylinder barrel, test the small-end and big-end bearings for wear. The gudgeon pin should be a free fit in the small-end bush, but it should not be possible to rock the gudgeon-pin by hand to any extent. Position the big-end at B.D.C. and see whether it is possible to move the connecting-rod up or down when firmly pushing and pulling on the connecting-rod in a vertical direction. No appreciable movement should be felt.

Dismantling the Flywheel Assembly. This requires very considerable skill and knowledge. The flywheels must run *dead true* when assembled and special equipment, including a dial indicator for testing true alignment and running, is required. Do not attempt to undertake dismantling and assembling the flywheel assembly yourself. Take the crankcase to an authorized Ariel repairer or deliver it to the maker's repair department for expert attention.

The Engine Shaft Shock-absorber. This is non-adjustable and the sliding member will function efficiently, provided that the two lock-nuts are kept tight against the spring-plate, which in turn will be locked against the shoulder of the driving shaft. If the unit is dismantled at any time, do not forget to replace the tab-washer *between* the lock-nuts, turning one tab over on to each respective nut.

CARE OF THE TRANSMISSION

The transmission on all Ariels comprises (front to rear): the primary chain, the clutch, the gearbox, and the secondary chain. It must be kept in an efficient condition to take full advantage of the high power-output Ariel engine.

Clutch Troubles. The two chief sources of trouble to which a clutch is prone are (*a*) clutch slip, and (*b*) clutch drag. The former can quickly be detected, as on opening the throttle suddenly the engine revolutions increase but the speed of the machine is not increased proportionately; also the clutch becomes very warm due to slip between the plates. Clutch slip may be due to oil getting on the clutch plates by over-filling the chain-case (*see* page 71). The remedy is to dismantle and clean the plates with petrol. Another possible cause of slip is insufficient clearance between the clutch operating lever and the plunger in the gearbox mainshaft. This trouble, which sometimes develops as the friction inserts become worn,

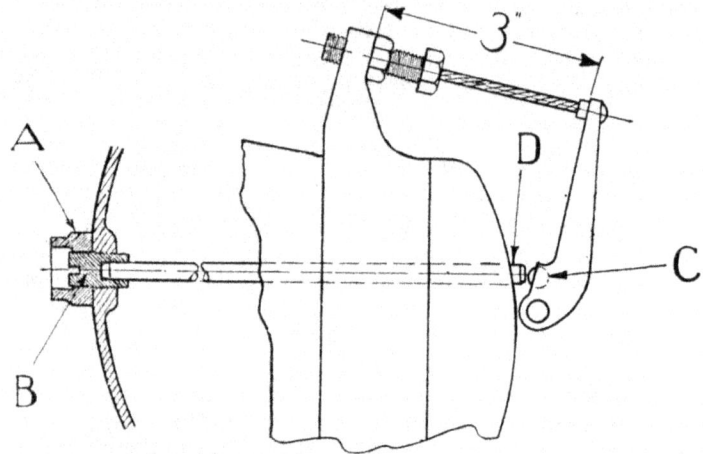

FIG. 68. BURMAN CLUTCH ADJUSTMENT (1939–49 250 C.C.)
Not applicable to 350 c.c. and 500 c.c. models

can easily be rectified by adjusting the clutch as described in later paragraphs.

Clutch drag, or difficulty in releasing the clutch, is also sometimes caused by oily plates, but the most likely cause of the trouble is incorrect clutch adjustment with excessive clearance between the operating lever and the plunger. A clutch which sticks when the machine has been left standing can be freed by depressing the kick-starter with the clutch raised before starting up the engine. A tipping spring-plate due to non-uniform spring pressure, and a worn clutch sprocket bearing are other possible causes of clutch drag, and the remedies are obvious.

To Adjust Clutch (1939–49 250 c.c. Models). To ensure freedom from slip it is essential that there is always about $\frac{1}{64}$ in. clearance between the ball (*C*) in the clutch-operating lever (*see* Fig. 68) and the end of the operating plunger (*D*). The lever must be set by means of the cable adjuster so that its end is approximately 3 in. from the face of the cable-adjuster lug on the gearbox. This setting gives equal movement of the actuating lever on each side of the centre line of its pivot with a minimum of bending of the wire cable. Then proceed to adjust the lock-nut (*A*) and adjuster (*B*) to give the necessary clearance. Slack off the lock-nut and rotate the adjuster (slotted end) with a screwdriver. To get at these parts it is, of course, necessary to take off the outer half of the oil-bath chaincase (except on oil-bath models where an inspection hole is provided in the clutch dome), but as the correct setting is given to the lever when the machine is assembled it will rarely be necessary to make this adjustment. In general, maintain at least $\frac{1}{64}$ in. clearance between the ball and the operating rod by adjusting the cable adjuster and give as straight a pull to the cable as possible.

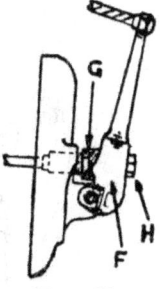

To Adjust Clutch (1939–51 350 c.c., 500 c.c., 600 c.c. Models). In the majority of cases the adjustment illustrated in Fig. 69 is used. A clearance of approximately $\frac{1}{64}$ in. should be maintained between the two thrust points on the lever (*F*) and the face of the plunger (*G*) which slides through the cover of the gearbox. To adjust the clearance, the top end of the operating lever should be pushed in and the cable slipped off. Then allow the lever to fall down, and rotate the screw (*H*) through the plunger anti-clockwise to increase the clearance or clockwise to decrease it. The cable may now be reconnected and the clearance carefully checked. If by any chance the plunger is removed, be very careful not to lose the small ball inserted between the end of the clutch rod and the adjuster screw (*H*). To remove the rubber protecting cover (1939 onwards) pull the top end down along the operating lever, after which the lever can be pushed in and the cable released.

FIG. 69.
BURMAN
CLUTCH
ADJUSTMENT
(1939–51
350–600 c.c.)

To Adjust Clutch (1952–60 "Magdyno" Models). To set the internal clutch operating-lever, slacken the small cover-plate secured by two screws to the face of the gearbox end-cover. Then adjust the sleeve nut by turning it, complete with the plate, until you find the correct position to give the required clearance. There should be $\frac{3}{16}$ in. free movement which can be felt after the oil filler plug is removed and the operating lever exposed. Finally remove all unnecessary slackness in the control cable by means of the external adjuster (i.e. the cable stop on top of the gearbox end-cover, or top end of the cable where Model VH is concerned). Be careful not to interfere with the operating-lever clearance already adjusted.

Clutch Springs Adjustment. Adjustment of the clutch plates and springs is rarely necessary, and all is correct as long as the spring nuts stand *level with the face of the spring plate*. After adjusting the clutch, see that the spring plate lifts equally; if not, the nuts should be eased off on the low side and tightened on the high side until it does.

To Adjust Clutch (1954–60 O.H.V. "Colts"). Clutch adjustment is seldom necessary, but referring to Fig. 70, check frequently that there is

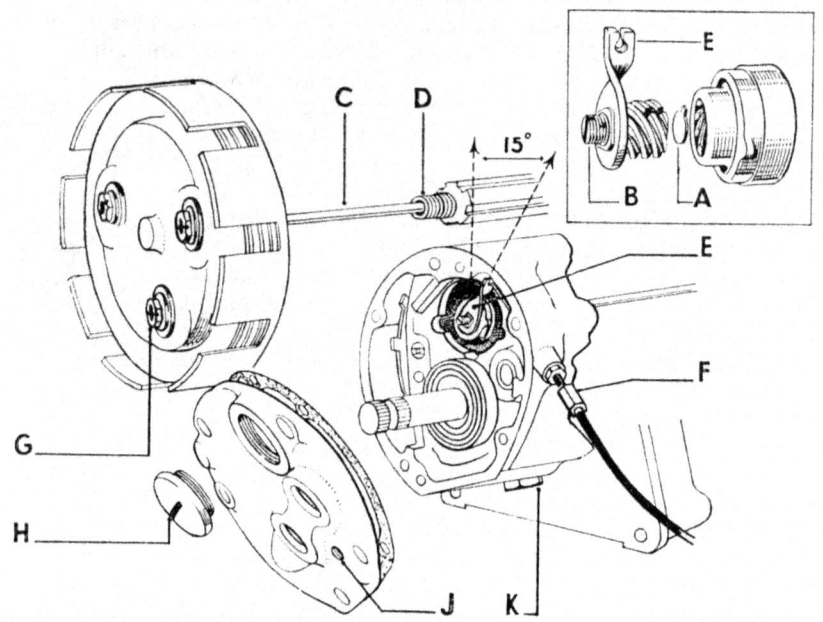

Fig. 70. Details of Burman Clutch Assembly on 1954–60 200 c.c. O.H.V. "Colts"

A. Steel thrust-plate
B. Centre screw
C. Push rod
D. Gearbox mainshaft
E. Operating lever
F. Control-cable adjuster
G. Clutch-spring lock-nut
H. Gearbox filler cap
J. Oil-level plug
K. Drain plug

at least $\frac{1}{16}$ in. free movement between the clutch operating-lever (E) and the push-rod (C). The operating lever (E) is set at an angle of approximately 15 degrees from the vertical and should not needlessly be altered because difficulty might be encountered in getting a satisfactory operating position. To obtain the normal running adjustment, adjust the control-cable adjuster (F). If further adjustment is required, turn the centre screw (B) *clockwise* to reduce movement, or anti-clockwise to increase it.

Note that if the clutch mechanism is dismantled at any time, be very careful to replace the hardened-steel thrust plate (A) in its correct position, otherwise damage may be caused to the end of the push-rod (C). Keep the three clutch-spring lock-nuts (*G*) screwed down tightly; these lock-nuts are not used for adjustment purposes.

Clutch Plate Removal (1952–60 "Magdyno" Models). Remove the clutch dome cover held by four screws and then undo the five spring retaining-nuts projecting through the end spring-plate. A slotted screwdriver is supplied in the tool kit for this purpose. The complete set of clutch plates can now be withdrawn from the housing. If clutch slip has taken place, carefully examine the condition of the cork (or fabric) inserts and replace with factory-exchange plates if necessary. Care should be taken when reassembling to fit the plates in the correct order. The first plate to put in is a plain one, then alternately a cork (or fabric) insert plate and a plain plate, finishing with a plain one.

Gearbox Trouble. Always keep it lubricated as described on page 69. Should gearbox trouble develop, this calls for dismantling of the gearbox and the author advises you to remove the complete gearbox from the frame and submit it to the nearest Ariel stockist, direct to the Service Department of Ariel Motors, Ltd., or to a qualified Burman gearbox repairer.

Primary Chain Adjustment (1939–60 "Magdyno" Models). Since the primary chain is automatically lubricated and totally enclosed, stretching takes considerably longer than is the case with the secondary chain, which is much more exposed to harmful influences. However, it will stretch in time, and it must be re-tensioned correctly. If a chain is too slack, it is apt to "whip," which intensifies the wear and tends to break the rollers, especially in the case of the front chain. On the other hand, if it is too tight, a crushing stress is produced on the rollers, and the whole chain is subjected to unfair stresses, and the sprockets wear quickly. The chain should be adjusted and kept adjusted, so that the chain (preferably the lower run) can be given a total and maximum deflection of about $\frac{3}{8}$ in. at the tightest point midway between the sprockets. The outer half of the oil-bath chain case can be removed to give access to the lower run of the chain. In many cases removal of the filter cap (1, Fig. 39) is sufficient to check chain tension.

Adjustment on all 1939 and later models (except 1939 250 c.c.) involves swinging the pivot-mounted Burman gearbox backwards or forwards as required by means of the adjusting device situated at the top rear extremity of the offside engine plate.

On 1939 and later models with a draw-bolt adjuster at the top-rear extremity of the off-side engine plate, to adjust the primary chain, slacken the pivot bolt below the gearbox and the clamp bolt above it. Then swing the gearbox about the pivot bolt by turning the nut on the draw bolt until correct chain tension is obtained. If the nut is found to be stiff, do not use undue force, otherwise the gearbox lug may be fractured. Find out what prevents the Burman gearbox from moving and check that the bolts are free and that the primary chain is not already taut. Finally re-tighten the pivot and clamp bolts. The latter must be thoroughly tightened, or the gearbox may move when the engine is pulling hard under heavy load. Afterwards check the tension of the secondary chain.

In the case of the 1939 250 c.c. Ariels the form of adjustment provided is similar to that on the larger models, but the clamp bolt is on the forward side of the gearbox and the draw bolt adjuster beneath the clamp bolt. To loosen the primary chain, slacken the pivot and clamp bolts. Then loosen the adjuster lock-nut above the stop on the engine plate and screw the lower lock-nut *upwards*. To tighten the chain, the lock-nut on the adjuster below the stop must be slackened and the upper lock-nut screwed *downwards*.

Primary Chain Adjustment (1954–60 O.H.V. "Colts"). As on the "Magdyno" models, adjustment is effected by moving the gearbox. Do not bother to remove the outer half of the oil-bath chain-case. Instead remove the filler cap and check the chain tension through its orifice. Rotate the engine slowly and, with the chain in several positions, check the up-and-down movement mid-way between the engine and clutch sprockets. With the chain in its tightest position, the maximum total deflection should not exceed $\frac{1}{2}$ in.

To make a chain adjustment, slacken the two long hexagon-headed sleeve nuts and serrated washers (located immediately below the gearbox on the off-side). Then carefully move the gearbox backwards and forwards as required until the chain tension (*see* above) is found to be correct. After re-tensioning the primary chain it is important to tighten the two hexagon-headed sleeve nuts very firmly, otherwise there is a likelihood of the engine thrust causing the gearbox to move forward and thereby slacken the chain. After adjusting the primary chain tension, check the tension of the secondary chain. Movement of the gearbox to the rear while making an adjustment usually slackens the secondary chain beyond the specified normal limits.

Secondary Chain Adjustment (Rigid-frame Models). On 1939–52 models with rigid-type frame, after re-tensioning the primary chain always check the tension of the secondary chain. Also do this at regular intervals, depending upon the mileage of the machine and how the rider has treated the chain. The chain in its tightest position should undergo a total maximum deflexion of about $\frac{5}{8}$ in. midway between the sprockets when properly adjusted. To adjust, loosen both rear-wheel spindle nuts (Fig. 71), slacken the rear brake adjuster, and screw up the two adjuster screws in the fork ends, after loosening the nut securing the brake anchor-bar. See that wheel alignment is not put out when tightening the adjusters, and also that the brake operation is not affected. Make whatever further adjustments are found necessary. Afterwards firmly re-tighten both adjuster screw lock-nuts and the two wheel-spindle nuts. Also tighten the brake anchor-bar securing nut. Finally, if in any doubt, check the alignment of the front and rear wheels.

Secondary Chain Adjustment (Models with Plunger-type Rear Suspension). On 1939–54 Ariels having plunger-type suspension (not "swinging

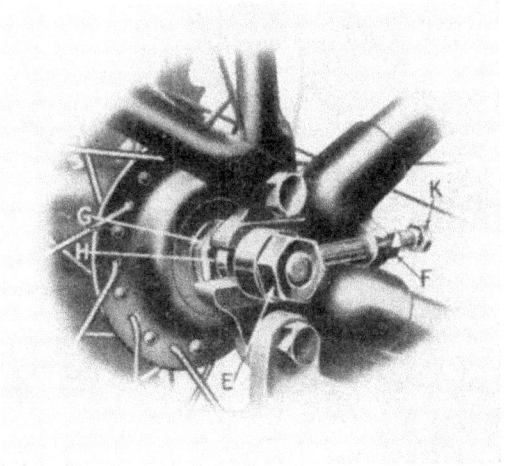

FIG. 71. SECONDARY CHAIN ADJUSTMENT (RIGID-FRAME MODELS)

K. Adjuster screw
F. Adjuster screw lock-nut
G. Bearing-adjuster nut

H. Lock-nut for G
E. Wheel-spindle nut

arm" models) a $\frac{3}{8}$ in. total and maximum chain deflexion (at the tightest point) is obtained not by two adjuster screws as on the rigid-frame models, but by means of two cams provided with integral hexagons. These cams are not inter-connected and therefore it is necessary after making a chain adjustment to check and if necessary adjust the alignment of the rear wheel.

On Ariels with non-detachable type wheels, slacken the two spindle outer nuts and the rear brake adjuster; then rotate both cams as required by using a suitable spanner applied to the cam hexagons. Afterwards re-tighten both spindle nuts firmly. Where a quickly-detachable wheel is fitted, first slacken the spindle nut on the near side and loosen the sleeve nut on the opposite side, that is, slacken it by applying a spanner to the centre of the three hexagons. The outer hexagon is part of the wheel-spindle bolt and the inner hexagon is integral with the cam adjuster. Both cams should be turned as required until correct chain adjustment is obtained. When this has been done the sleeve nut and spindle bolt should be firmly tightened by means of their hexagons. Do not forget to check the adjustment of the rear brake.

Secondary Chain Adjustment ("Swinging Arm" Models). On 1954–60 models with "swinging arm" rear suspension the design for the chain adjustment does not include cams as on the machines previously referred to, and the means of adjustment is similar to that provided for the earlier

FIG. 72. SECONDARY CHAIN ADJUSTMENT ("SWINGING ARM" MODELS)
1. Chain inspection-hole plug
2. Wheel-spindle nut
3. Lock-nut for 4
4. Adjuster screw
5. Rubber plug for hole giving access to hub-securing nuts

rigid-frame models. After adjusting the primary chain, and at regular intervals (depending on mileage and riding tactics) check the tension of the chain with the motor-cycle on its centre stand and the *damper units fully extended*.

Remove the rubber inspection-hole plug shown at (1) in Fig. 72 and move the chain up and down by hand. With the chain in its tightest position there should be a total deflexion of between $1\frac{1}{4}$ in. and $1\frac{1}{2}$ in. Note that this will give a normal adjustment of $\frac{5}{8}$ in. up-and-down movement when the rear wheel rests on the ground and you are seated on the dualseat.

Referring to Fig. 72, to adjust the secondary chain, slacken off the two rear-wheel spindle nuts (2), slacken the rear brake adjuster, and loosen the nut securing the brake anchor-bar to the brake plate. Then carefully and evenly turn the chain-tension adjuster screws (4) clockwise. It is most important to turn each adjuster screw exactly the same amount, otherwise wheel alignment is upset and must be checked. After making the necessary adjustment, firmly tighten the wheel-spindle nuts, the lock-nuts on the adjuster screws, and the brake anchor-bar nut. Finally check the adjustment of the rear brake.

Secondary Chain Adjustment (1954–60 O.H.V. "Colts"). On the 200 c.c. "Colts" the form of adjustment provided is similar to that used on pedal

FIG. 73. SECONDARY CHAIN ADJUSTMENT (O.H.V. "COLTS")
This illustration also shows the rear-brake adjustment and details of the plunger-type rear suspension

cycles, as may be observed in Fig. 73. With the lower chain run in its tightest position there should be a total up-and-down deflexion, midway between the sprockets, of $\frac{1}{2}$ in. An adjustment is likely to be necessary after re-tensioning the primary chain, and at intervals through wear and lengthening of the secondary chain. Should an adjustment be required, effect this as described below.

Place your "Colt" on its centre stand, with the rear wheel in its lowest position in the rear-suspension units. Referring to Fig. 73, slacken off the rear brake adjuster (1), otherwise free movement of the rear wheel backwards may be hindered. Also slacken the rear-wheel spindle nuts (2) on both sides of the motor-cycle, so as to provide easy movement of the spindle in the rear-fork ends. Now turn slowly and evenly the two adjuster nuts (3) on both sides and draw the rear wheel backwards the necessary amount to give a secondary-chain deflexion of $\frac{5}{8}$ in. Equal tightening of the nuts is essential to maintain true wheel alignment. Tighten firmly the two rear-wheel spindle nuts and screw the rear-brake adjuster forwards as required to give normal brake operation. If in any doubt about wheel alignment, check this. Lack of true alignment accelerates tyre wear and gives imperfect steering.

WHEELS, BRAKES, AND TYRES

To Remove Front Wheel (1939–46 Models with Girder Forks). First place the machine on the rear stand, lift up the front wheel and push over the front stand just forward of the vertical position. Make sure, however,

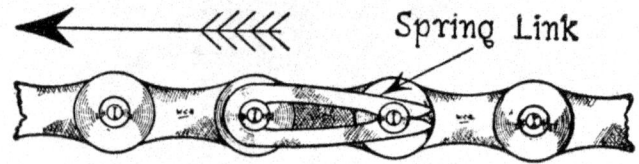

FIG. 74. SEE THAT YOUR CHAIN SPRING LINK IS FITTED LIKE THIS
For safety this is essential. A chain is best joined on a sprocket

that the stand does not foul the brake-cam bearing. Next detach the bolt from the upper end of the brake anchor-bar. Also if the speedometer is driven off the front wheel, disconnect its cable at the bottom end. Now slacken the two wheel spindle nuts, slip the washers out of the front fork recesses and allow the front wheel to come away.

To Remove Front Wheel (1947–55 Telescopic Forks). First jack up the machine on both stands. Clean all dirt from the exposed portion of the front-wheel spindle, between the fork-tube lug on the opposite side to the brake, and the wheel itself. Then unscrew the nut from the front-wheel spindle. Also unscrew the bolt which secures the brake plate to the off-side fork-leg. Now rotate the brake plate slightly until the cable nipple is able to be detached from the brake lever. Next loosen the pinch-bolt, located on the other fork tube, and with a suitable tommy-bar, inserted through the hole on the near-side, pull the wheel spindle straight out. When doing this, give the spindle a slight twist in either direction. Finally ease the front wheel from the telescopic forks and plug the spindle holes to prevent the entry of dirt. The foregoing instructions do not apply to "Colts."

Removing Front Wheel (1956–60 Telescopic Forks). On "Magdyno" models, follow these instructions. Jack your Ariel up on its front and centre stands. Next release the front-brake cable from the stop lug. Also release the off-side front-mudguard stay and the brake plate anchor-bar. Now slacken the pinch-bolt on the lower end of the near-side fork tube, and remove the large hub-spindle nut on the brake-plate side. Finally insert a tommy-bar in the hole on the end of the hub spindle. Turn it in either direction, and pull out the spindle. The front wheel can now be withdrawn.

Removing Front Wheel (1954-60 O.H.V. "Colts"). With the machine on its centre stand, uncouple the front-brake cable, first at the lever on the

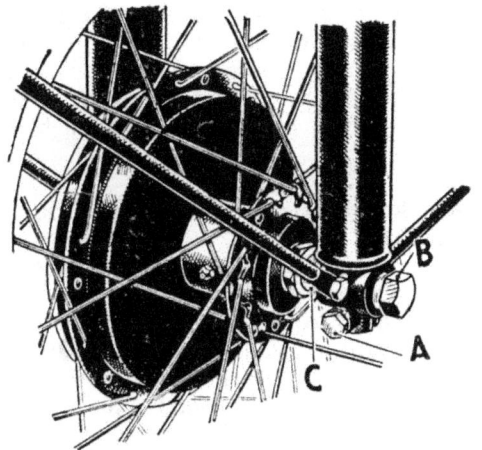

FIG. 75. REMOVAL OF THE FRONT WHEEL
Applicable to 200 c.c. "Colt" engines only

brake cover-plate, and then by unscrewing it from the top. Referring to Fig. 75, loosen the pinch-bolt (*A*) and unscrew the wheel spindle by applying a spanner to its head (*B*). This spindle has a *left-hand* thread; therefore unscrew it *clockwise*. Remove the spindle from the near-side. Observe that the spindle fits into the bush (*C*) which registers in the fork end. When withdrawing the spindle, support the weight of the front wheel by hand, and push the bush outwards through the fork end as far as is practicable. This provides sufficient clearance for the front wheel to be withdrawn.

Assembling Front Wheel (1939-46 Models with Girder Forks). Assemble the front wheel in the reverse order of dismantling.

To Assemble Front Wheel (1947-55 Telescopic Forks). Replace the front wheel in the reverse order of dismantling. Before tightening the pinch-bolt work the forks up and down once or twice by pressing on the handlebars to allow the end lug to find its natural position along the spindle. Tighten the pinch-bolt in this position, being careful not to move the lug along the spindle while doing so.

Assembling Front Wheel (1956–60 Telescopic Forks). Assemble in the reverse order of removal.

To Assemble Front Wheel (1954–60 O.H.V. "Colts"). Replace the front wheel in the reverse order of removal. Make sure that the stud in the brake cover-plate fits properly in its socket, otherwise the brake will fail to function. Before tightening the pinch-bolt (A, Fig. 75) depress the forks sharply several times to enable the near-side fork lug to align itself on the spindle. Failure to take this precaution may result in the fork leg being incorrectly aligned and trouble will ensue. Re-tighten the pinch-bolt securely.

To Adjust Front-wheel Bearings (1939–46). The taper roller-bearings are adjustable. Referring to Fig. 71, to effect an adjustment, loosen the wheel-spindle outer nut (E). Then hold the bearing cone-adjuster nut (G) with a thin spanner, and loosen the outer lock-nut (H). Carefully adjust the bearing by means of the inner nut (G) until there is just the *slightest* amount of bearing slackness as measured at the wheel rim. Having made the necessary adjustment of the inner nut, avoid moving it again while tightening the lock-nut (H) and outer nut (G).

Journal-type Front-wheel Bearings. Note that on all 1947–8 Ariels with telescopic front forks (except the 1954–9 "Colts") the journal-type roller bearings have *no adjustment*.

Adjusting Front-wheel Bearings (1954–60 O.H.V. "Colts"). The 200 c.c. coil-ignition models have ball bearings of the cup and cone type, and these can be adjusted with the front wheel removed in the following manner. Slacken the outer lock-nut on the near-side of the hub and then tighten or loosen the adjacent inner nut as required to obtain a *just perceptible* side play at the rim. Having obtained the correct adjustment, re-tighten the outer lock-nut against the (inner) adjuster nut. Afterwards make a final check on the adjustment.

To Remove Non-detachable Rear Wheel (Rigid Frame). On 1939–52 rigid-frame models the procedure for rear-wheel removal is generally the same as for front-wheel removal on 1939–46 models with girder-type front forks (*see* page 128), except for a few slight variations. Jack your Ariel up on its rear stand and proceed to disconnect the rear-brake rod, the secondary chain, and the brake anchor-plate bar. Swing up the hinged

GENERAL MAINTENANCE   131

portion of the rear mudguard, unscrew both spindle nuts, and withdraw the rear wheel clear of the fork ends. Check wheel alignment after replacing the wheel.

Removing Quickly-detachable Rear Wheel (Rigid Frame). On 1939–52 rigid-frame Ariels place the machine on its rear stand and swing up the rear portion of the rear mudguard. Then unscrew the three nuts which secure the wheel hub to the brake drum. Next loosen the pair of plated stay nuts and unscrew and remove the spindle bolt on the right-hand side of the wheel. Now tap out the distance sleeve between the hollow wheel-spindle and the right-hand fork. It may have already fallen out. Pull the rear wheel to the right-hand side until it is quite clear of the driving pegs and studs, and lift it away from the machine. To replace the quickly-detachable rear wheel, follow the reverse procedure. Also check wheel alignment.

To Remove Quickly-detachable Rear Wheel (Plunger-type Rear Suspension). On 1939–54 models with rear suspension the removal procedure is the same as previously described for the rigid-frame models. The detachable-spindle bolt is mounted in a sleeve in the rear-fork end and this sleeve carries the cam-type adjustment for rectifying slackness in the secondary chain. Removal of the quickly-detachable wheel does *not* upset the alignment of the wheel or the adjustment of the chain.

Removing Non-detachable Rear Wheel (Plunger-type Rear Suspension). Instructions for removing the non-detachable type wheel on models provided with rear springing are also exactly the same as those for rigid-frame models, referred to on page 130. It should, however, be borne in mind that with the non-detachable wheel the two cam adjusters come away with the rear wheel during its removal. Therefore chain adjustment and wheel alignment are upset, necessitating readjustment and realignment during assembly.

Removing Quickly-detachable Rear Wheel ("Swinging Arm" Models). On 1954–60 "Magdyno" models with "swinging arm" rear suspension, to remove the rear wheel, first place the machine on its centre stand. Remove the brake cable from the operating lever and adjuster on the brake plate after turning the latter and also the lock-nut until the "split" permits the inner wire to be withdrawn. Disconnect the secondary chain and remove the securing bolt from the front end of the brake anchor-bar.

Remove the rubber plug shown at (5) in Fig. 72 from the chain-case (where fitted), which completely encloses the secondary chain. Then slowly turn the rear wheel to expose in turn each of the four hub securing-nuts. Remove each of these nuts by inserting the spanner provided in the tool kit through the rubber-plug orifice. Now withdraw the hub-spindle bolt illustrated in Fig. 76.

Remove both bolts securing the stays which hold the dualseat, and also the four bolts securing the rear end of the mudguard. Detach the two rear-lamp "snap" cable-connectors inside the rear guard, and the rear end of the mudguard can now be removed. This facilitates the easy removal of the complete wheel and leaves the secondary chain, chain

FIG. 76. REMOVAL OF QUICKLY-DETACHABLE REAR WHEEL (1954–60)
Not applicable to 1954–60 Ariel "Colts"

sprocket and the short fixed-spindle (*see* Fig. 76) in position. It is *not* necessary to check the wheel alignment after assembly.

NOTE: When replacing the wheel spindle, it is simpler to engage the thread if the N/s nut is slackened about *one turn*. Should you remove the brake anchor-plate, note that it is not absolutely flat, the large end pointing very slightly inwards and the smaller end outwards. Be very careful when reassembling to fit the anchor plate correctly. Also when greasing the bearings (*see* page 73) avoid excessive grease, or some may exude on to the brake linings.

To Remove Rear Wheel (O.H.V. "Colts"). To remove the rear wheel on 1954–60 coil-ignition "Colt" models, first unscrew the speedometer cable where it enters the rear-hub gearing. Next disconnect the secondary chain by removing its spring link (*see* Fig. 74) and unwind the chain from the rear-wheel sprocket. Leave the chain still in position on the gearbox sprocket. Unscrew the hand adjuster (1, Fig. 73) on the rear-brake rod completely. Slacken off the rear-wheel spindle nuts (2, Fig. 73) sufficiently to enable the rear wheel to be withdrawn. It is advisable to check wheel alignment after assembly.

The Rear-wheel Bearings. Ball journals are provided for the hub bearings on all 1947–60 models (including O.H.V. "Colts") and no adjustment is included or necessary. On 1939–46 rigid-frame models with girder-type front forks, however, an adjustment is provided for the rear-wheel bearings. The adjustment procedure is the same as that described on page 130 for the front-wheel bearings of 1939–46 models.

Front Brake Adjustment (1939–46). Adjust as required by means of the knurled adjuster on the end of the cable stop.

To Adjust Front Brake (1947–55). On 1947–55 "Magdyno" models having telescopic-type front forks, take up initial cable stretch by adjusting the cable stop. Afterwards compensate for brake lining wear by turning the square-ended cam (attached to the brake plate) as required. This adjustment is similar to that provided for the rear brake. When making an adjustment, turn the cam one or more "clicks" in a *clockwise* direction.

Front Brake Adjustment (1956–60). Fitted to the handlebars of all "Magdyno" Ariels is a knurled screw located on the brake lever, which can be used for adjusting the cable tension, and taking up the initial cable stretch. Adjustment for brake-lining wear is made by turning the square-ended cam, or fulcrum screw, with the special spanner provided.

The cable should first be slackened off as far as possible, and then the brake shoes adjusted by turning the fulcrum screw *clockwise* until the shoes just touch the cable drum. Release the fulcrum screw 2 or 3 notches, until the wheel revolves freely, and then re-tension the brake cable with the knurled screw.

To Adjust Front Brake (1954–60 O.H.V. "Colts"). When an adjustment is necessary, alter the length of the brake cable at its lower end by means of a knurled thumb-nut on the cable stop.

Rear Brake Adjustment (Rigid Frame). On 1939–52 rigid-frame Ariels diametrically opposite to the brake lever bearing is a fulcrum screw (*see* Fig. 77) for adjusting the rear brake. To make an adjustment in order to compensate for wear of the brake linings, first slacken off the thumb screw on the rear end of the brake rod. Then turn the square-ended fulcrum screw *clockwise* to compensate for lining wear. When no further turning is possible, the thumb screw on the brake rod must be re-tightened so as to provide only a very slight amount of idle movement of the rear brake pedal.

Never use the thumb screw except to compensate for secondary chain adjustment. All normal brake adjustment should *always* be made by means

FIG. 77. REAR BRAKE ADJUSTMENT (1939–52 RIGID FRAME)
This view also shows the secondary chain adjustment

of the fulcrum screw on the brake plate. This ensures the maximum brake efficiency being obtained.

To Adjust Rear Brake (1939–53 Plunger-type Rear Suspension). On 1939–53 Ariels having plunger-type rear suspension, adjust the rear brake as just described for rigid-frame models (*see* Fig. 77). First make the necessary fulcrum-screw adjustment and then adjust, if required, the thumb screw on the brake rod. It should be observed that on the spring-frame models the brake plate has no lock-nut securing it to the spindle. Collars inside and outside the brake plate locate the latter axially. When the wheel-spindle nuts are firmly tightened, the brake plate is securely gripped and held. A peg on the stirrup engages a slot in the brake plate and prevents the latter from rotating during brake application. It is important to verify that the peg and slot *are* in engagement when replacing the rear wheel.

GENERAL MAINTENANCE 135

Adjustment of Brake Pedal. Always complete brake adjustment by means of the thumb screw on the rear brake rod so that there is the *minimum* of lost motion when the brake pedal is operated. This ensures powerful and sensitive braking.

Rear Brake Adjustment (1954–5 S.V. Models). On all S.V. models (Model VB) an unusual type of rear-brake assembly (*see* Fig. 78) is provided. Effect all normal brake adjustment by means of the square-ended

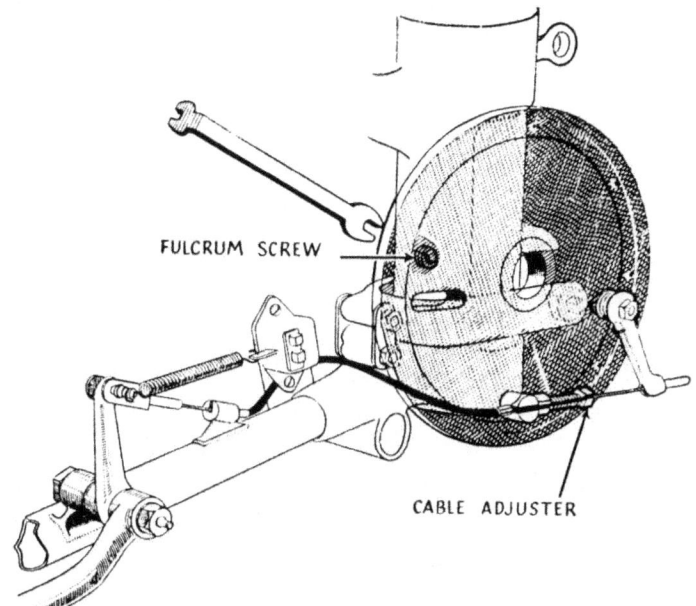

FIG. 78. CABLE-OPERATED REAR BRAKE (1954–5 S.V.)
This assembly applies only to the 600 c.c. Model VB

fulcrum screw in the brake plate. To compensate for wear on the brake linings, turn the screw *clockwise*. Use the cable adjuster only to take up slack in the flexible brake cable and also to position the brake pedal to give a slight degree of free movement.

To Adjust Rear Brake (1954–5 O.H.V. "Red Hunters"). The "swinging arm" O.H.V. models have a rear-brake arrangement rather similar to that on the S.V. models just referred to. From Fig. 79, however, it will be noted that a brake pedal adjustable stop is provided and the positions of the fulcrum screw and the cable adjuster are different.

Follow the instructions just given for the 1954–5 side-valve models, but also set the adjustable brake-pedal stop to give the pedal the best

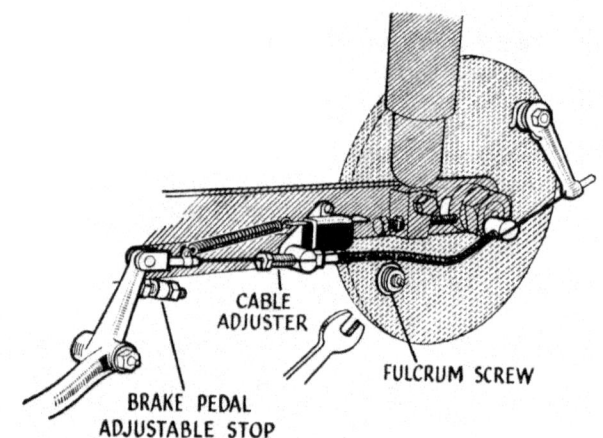

Fig. 79. Cable-operated Rear Brake (1954–5 O.H.V.)
This arrangement applies only to the 350 and 500 c.c. Models NH, VH

Fig. 80. Cable-operated Rear Brake (1956–60 S.V., O.H.V.)
On "swinging arm" models with full-width hubs the rear-brake pedal is located on the near-side and the cable control on the off-side as shown

riding position to suit the individual rider. Afterwards firmly tighten the lock-nut.

Adjusting Rear Brake (All 1956–60 Models). All 1956–60 Ariel "swinging arm" S.V. and O.H.V. models have a cable-operated rear brake, and because of the inclusion of a full-width light-alloy hub, the operating lever, cable, cable-adjuster screw, and fulcrum screw are all positioned on the off-side as shown in Fig. 80.

To adjust the rear brake, first slacken off fully the cable adjuster and then adjust the brake shoes by turning the fulcrum screw *clockwise* until the brake linings just touch the bearing surface of the brake drum. Now release the fulcrum screw two or three notches, until the rear wheel rotates freely. Finally re-tension the brake cable with the cable adjuster, leaving just a trace of free movement.

To Adjust Rear Brake (1954–60 O.H.V. "Colts"). Adjust the rear hub to give maximum efficiency and good control by means of the finger adjustment provided at the end of the brake rod.

To Obtain Good Tyre Mileage. Always maintain the correct tyre pressures and keep the wheels in alignment. Avoid fierce acceleration, violent braking, and stunt cornering. Handle the clutch gently, remove flints which bed into the cover, and keep oil or paraffin from the treads.

Maintaining Correct Tyre Pressures. Over-inflation causes vibration, strains the cover, and can cause concussion bursts; under-inflation produces a tendency for tyre creep, rolling, instability of steering, and cracking of the cover. All of these things are objectionable and you should therefore always run with the tyres inflated to the correct pressures and check the pressures weekly with a pressure gauge. Suitable tyre pressure-gauges are the Holdtite, the Dunlop pencil-type No. 6, the Schrader 7750, and the Romac. About once a year valve "insides" should be replaced. They can be removed by taking off each valve cap and using its slotted end as a screwdriver. See that both valve caps are fitted and kept firmly tightened. This is important.

Table VII shows the minimum tyre-inflation pressures recommended for tyres fitted to 1939–60 Ariels. These pressures are based on a rider's weight of 176 lb. For riders whose weight exceeds 176 lb, increase the pressures slightly. Add 1 lb per sq in. for every 28 lb increase in weight above 176 lb, in the case of the front tyre. Where the rear tyre is concerned, add 1 lb per sq in. for every 14 lb increase in weight above 176 lb. Should an extra load be carried in the form of a pillion passenger or luggage, determine the actual load on each tyre (preferably on a weighbridge at a railway station or large transport depot) and then use the minimum tyre pressure recommended in Table VIII.

TABLE VII
RECOMMENDED INFLATION PRESSURES FOR DUNLOP TYRES ON S.V., O.H.V. SINGLES (1939–60)
(In lb per sq. in.)

Ariel Model (Type No.)	Front Tyre		Rear Tyre		Sidecar Tyre
	3·00–20	3·25–19	3·25–19	3·50–19	3·25–19
Solo					
VH, NH	22	18	24	19	—
VG, NG / VA, VB	—	18	24	20	—
OH, OG	20	16	22	18	—
LH	—	16	27	—	—
Sidecar					
VH, NH	26	18	28	24	17
VG, NG / VA, VB	—	22	28	24	17

TABLE VIII
MINIMUM TYRE PRESSURES FOR SPECIFIC LOADS

Nominal Tyre Section (in.)	Inflation Pressures (lb per sq. in.)					
	16	18	20	24	28	32
	Load per Tyre (lb)					
2·375	120	140	160	185	210	240
2·50	120	140	160	185	210	240
2·75	140	160	180	210	250	280
3·00	160	180	200	240	300	350
3·25	200	240	280	350	400	440
3·50	280	320	350	400	450	500
4·00	360	400	430	500	—	—

(*By courtesy of The Dunlop Rubber Co., Ltd.*)

GENERAL MAINTENANCE

Wheel Alignment. To obtain maximum tyre life, good steering, and safe riding on wet roads, it is very important to keep both wheels always truly aligned. After removing a rear wheel (except a quickly-detachable type), or adjusting the secondary chain, check that the wheel alignment *is* correct.

Place a straight-edge or a board alongside the front and rear wheels. Assuming that both tyres are of the same section, the wood should, of course, contact both tyres at four points. If one tyre is of larger section than the other, make due allowance for this. Some riders (including myself) check the alignment with a taut piece of string having its front end attached by a nail or screw to an anchorage post such as a fence or tree. If reasonable care is taken, this is quite a satisfactory method of checking wheel alignment. Should the alignment be found incorrect, with the handlebars in their normal position, make the necessary adjustment with the secondary-chain adjusters (*see* pages 124–8).

Where a sidecar is attached, the sidecar wheel should "toe-in" approximately 1 in. and the motor-cycle itself should *lean slightly outwards away from the sidecar.* The exact dimensions vary slightly according to the design of sidecar fitted, and the maker's instructions should be closely followed.

STEERING HEAD AND SUSPENSION

Steering-head Adjustment (1939–46 Girder Forks). This should be such that it allows perfect freedom without up-and-down play. To test this, stand astride the machine and grip the bars. Lift them to ascertain if any movement is felt.

Before adjusting the cup and cone ball bearings, remove the weight from the front wheel by supporting the crankcase with a suitable block. The steering damper should also be slackened right off. Now loosen the bolt passing through the ball-head clip and unscrew a few turns the thin lock-nut placed over the adjuster nut above the clip. The adjuster nut can then be screwed up until all "shake" in the handlebars is eliminated, but avoid over-tightening the nut. Finally, lock the adjustment by means of the lock-nut and check the adjustment once again.

To Adjust Steering Head (1947–60 Telescopic Forks). Within certain limits automatic adjustment of the steering-head ball races is provided. If slackness in the steering-head bearings (on a "Magdyno" model) develops after the first few hundred miles and then at very infrequent intervals, rectify in the following manner.

Support the front of your Ariel by placing a box beneath the crankcase. With the front wheel clear of the ground, slacken the top lock-nut and gradually screw the bottom nut down until all steering head slackness has just disappeared and there is no stiffness. Then further tighten the bottom nut $\frac{1}{6}$ of a turn (i.e. from one pair of flats on the hexagon to the next pair).

Finally re-tighten the top lock-nut. While doing this, apply a second spanner to the bottom lock-nut to prevent its turning.

Steering Head Adjustment (1954–60 O.H.V. "Colts"). On the 200 c.c. coil-ignition models it is recommended that the steering head be checked for play about every 1,000 miles. To do this, raise the machine and insert a box beneath the crankcase sufficient to lift the front wheel clear of the ground. Stand astride your "Colt" and grip the handlebars firmly while

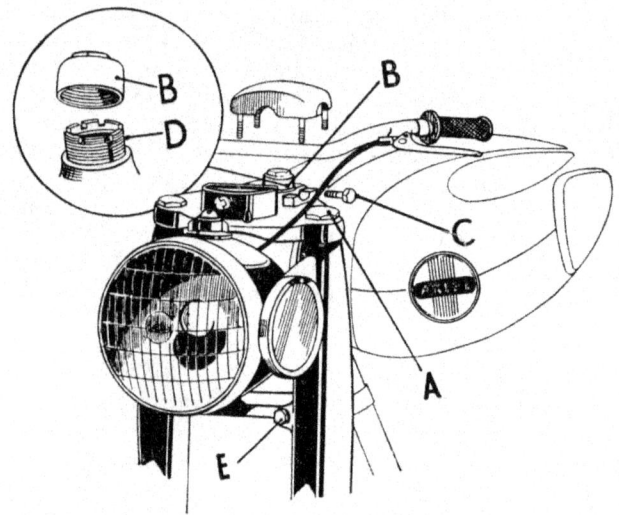

FIG. 81. STEERING HEAD ADJUSTMENT (1954–60 O.H.V. "COLTS")

applying up-and-down movement. No slackness should be felt. At the same time check that the steering head is quite free (i.e. that the ball-race adjustment is not too close).

Referring to Fig. 81, to effect an adjustment, remove the steering head lock-nut (*B*) and slacken the pinch-bolt (*C*). Also slacken the two pinch-bolts (*E*) which are located close to where the front-fork legs pass through the lower steering-yoke; these bolts must be freed so that during the adjustment of the steering column the yoke can take up a new position.

Turn the adjuster sleeve (*D*) until all slackness (up-and-down play) disappears. Be careful not to overtighten the sleeve (*D*), otherwise the steering will be stiff and damage may be caused to the ball race. Afterwards tighten all three pinch-bolts and the lock-nut (*B*), and again check the adjustment.

Plunger-type Rear Suspension (1939–54). Referring to Fig. 82, occasionally check the lower domed-nut for tightness. No other attention is normally necessary, except for greasing (*see* page 74) of the two nipples shown. After a very big mileage it may be desirable to effect bush renewal, and this is best done by a motor-cycle repairer who handles Ariels, but you can do the job yourself if careful.

Plunger-type Rear Suspension (1954–60). On the 200 c.c. O.H.V. "Colts" no maintenance whatever is normally required except for regular greasing of the single nipple provided on each suspension unit.

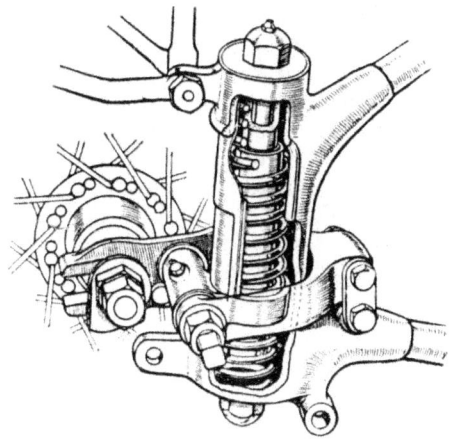

Fig. 82. Rear Suspension Unit (1939–54)
Observe the two grease nipples

"Swinging Arm" Rear Suspension. For all practical purposes you can disregard both the sealed units and the "swinging arm" pivot (*see* page 74).

Telescopic Front Forks (1947–60). You can also forget these unless after a very big mileage some excessive up-and-down movement occurs. The remedy for this trouble is to replenish the forks with the correct lubricant (*see* pages 75–6). Internal components of the forks wear very slowly unless rough riding over rough ground is foolishly indulged in.

Girder-type Front Forks (1939–46). Forks of the non-telescopic type *do* require some periodical attention. Greasing is dealt with on page 76. No side play should exist in the fork links and to obtain satisfactory and safe suspension the front forks should have a free action, with just sufficient friction in the fork links to prevent excessive fork bounce on wavy roads.

To make an adjustment of the spindles, slacken the two hexagon locknuts, one at each end of the spindle, and rotate the spindle by means of a spanner placed on the squared end. An *anti-clockwise* rotation tightens the links. It should be noted that re-tightening the lock-nut at the end which is not squared will tighten up the adjustment; therefore adjust a little at a time, screw up the lock-nut, and test. If the adjustment is not right, it is necessary to repeat the process until the correct adjustment is obtained. Finally re-tighten the lock-nut at the squared end.

The reason that the tightening up of the lock-nut affects the adjustment is that the spindle at this end is stepped, the shoulder bearing up against a corresponding shoulder in the hole through the link. When the lock-nut is loosened, the link moves away from the shoulder on the spindle and extra clearance therefore develops. For correct spindle adjustment the forks should move freely with the dampers out of action, and with no side play in the links. The knurled washers near the side links serve as a good guide to correct adjustment. These should just rotate easily.

To bring the fork dampers into action, adjust the spindle which passes through the damper discs, as already described.

The fork dampers are adjusted by means of the hand nut on the off-side lower front spindle only. Maintain the spindle screwed right home in the near-side link and the lock-nut tight. The auxiliary damper-springs fitted on 1946 Ariels require no attention.

INDEX

ACCESSORY firms, 77
Air filter, 29
Alignment, headlamp, 39
Alternator, Wipac, 47, 50
Amal carburettor—
  functioning of, 19–23
  maintenance, 26–9
  tuning, 24–6
Ammeter, 34
Automatic advance mechanism, 87

BALL valves, oil pump, 55, 63
Battery—
  filler, Lucas, 36
  maintenance, 34–8
Brake—
  adjustment, 133–7
  lubrication, 74
  operation, 15
Brushes, dynamo, 31
Bulb renewal, 41–2, 49–50

CARBON removal, 102–3
Carburettor—
  functioning of, 19–23
  maintenance, 26–9
  settings, 24
  tuning, 24–6
Central stand, 76
Cleaning—
  chromium, 79
  contacts, 85
  enamel, 79
  engine and gearbox, 78
  Lucas lamps, 41
  sparking plug, 81–3
Clutch—
  adjustment, 120–3
  lubrication, 70
  springs, 121
  troubles, 119
Commutator, 32
Compensated voltage control, 33
Connecting-rod bearings, 119

Contact-breaker—
  gap, 83–5
  lubrication, 67–8
Controls, 3–6, 7, 9
C.V.C. unit terminals, 32
Cylinder—
  barrel removal, 96, 97, 100
  replacing, 107–8
  head removal, 95–8

DECARBONIZING, 93–111
Dynamo—
  maintenance, 30–4
  removal, 33

ENGINE—
  assembly, final, 108–11
  lubrication systems, 54–8
  oil, changing, 64
  oils, suitable, 58
  shaft shock-absorber, 119
  trouble chart, 12
Exhaust-valve lifter adjustment, 92
Exide battery, 49

FILTERS, cleaning, 64–6
Flat battery, Wipac, 53
Flywheel assembly, 119
Focusing, 39
Footrest adjustment, 3
Front forks, 74–6, 141–2

GAP—
  contact-breaker, 83–5
  sparking plug, 81
Gear—
  change indicator, 13–14
  changing, 12–15
Gearbox—
  lubrication, 69
  troubles, 123
Girder-type front forks, 141
Greases, suitable, 73
Grinding-in valves, 105
Gudgeon-pin removal, 100

HILL climbing, 15
Horns, Lucas, 46
Hydrometer, Lucas, 37

IGNITION—
lever, 5
switch, 5
timing, 111–14

JET needle position, 25

KICK-STARTING, 10–11

LICENCES, 1
Lighting switch positions, 39
Lubrication—
clutch, 70
engine, 54–68
front forks, 74–6
gearbox, 69
"Magdyno," 67
primary chain, 70
rear suspension, 74
rocker-box, 67
secondary chain, 71
speedometer gearbox, 74
steering head, 73
systems, 54–8
wheel bearings, 73
Wipac contact-breaker, 68
Lucas—
horns, 46
lamps, 39–42

"MAGDYNO"—
chain tension, 114
contact-breaker, 83
lubrication, 67
Maintenance, items for, 77

OIL—
circulation, checking, 59, 61
consumption, heavy, 62
level in tank, 59
pipes, 66
pressure fluctuation, 61
gauge, 59
readings, 11
regulator, 59
valve, 61

Oil (contd.)—
pump, assembling, 118
purifier, 63
replenishment, 6
tank filter, 65

PETROL tank removal, 93–5
Pilot jet, obstructed, 26
Piston—
removal, 100
replacing, 107
rings, 101
Preliminaries, 1
Primary chain—
adjustment, 123–4
lubrication, 70

REAR suspension, 74, 140–1
Rectifier, Wipac, 47
Replenishment, 6
Riding position, 3
Rocker-box lubrication, 67
Rocker-boxes, dismantling, 118
Running-in, 16, 58

SADDLE nose-bolt, 74
Secondary chain—
adjustment, 124–8
lubrication, 71
Sidecar, attaching, 18
Slow-running adjustment, 24–6
Spares and repairs, 77
Sparking plugs, recommended, 80
Specific gravity of electrolyte, 37
Spring arm, "Magdyno," 86
Starting up, 7–11
Steering—
damper, 17
head adjustment, 139–40
lubrication, 73
lock, 17
Stopping, 15–16
Storage of battery, 38
Sump filter, 65

TAPPET adjustment, S.V., 88
Testing sparking plug, 83
Timing—
ignition, 111–14
valve, 115–18

INDEX

Topping-up battery, 34
Tuning carburettor, 24–6
Tyre pressures, 137–8

VALVE—
  clearances, 87–91
  fitting, 106
  removing, 103–5
  springs, 106
  timing, 115–18
Varley battery, 48

WHEEL—
  bearings, lubricating, 73
  removal, 128–33
Wipac—
  alternator, 47, 50
  contact-breaker, 85
Wiring—
  diagrams, 44–6, 51, 52
  Lucas equipment, 43–5

YALE keys, 17

OTHER MOTORCYCLE MANUALS AVAILABLE IN THIS SERIES

AJS (BOOK OF) ALL MODELS 1955-1965:
350cc & 500cc Singles ~ Models 16, 16S, 18, 18S

ARIEL WORKSHOP MANUAL 1933-1951:
All single, twin & 4 cylinder models

ARIEL (BOOK OF) MAINTENANCE & REPAIR MANUAL 1932-1939:
LF3, LF4, LG, NF3, NF4, NG, OG, VA, VA3, VA4, VB, VF3, VF4, VG, Red Hunter LH, NH, OH, VH & Square Four 4F, 4G, 4H

BMW FACTORY WORKSHOP MANUAL R27, R28:
English, German, French and Spanish text

BMW FACTORY WORKSHOP MANUAL R50, R50S, R60, R69S:
Also includes a supplement for the USA models: R50US, R60US, R69US. English, German, French and Spanish text

BSA PRE-WAR SINGLES & TWINS (BOOK OF) 1936-1939:
All Pre-War single & twin cylinder SV & OHV models through 1939
150cc, 250cc, 350cc, 500cc, 600cc, 750cc & 1,000cc

BSA SINGLES (BOOK OF) 1945-1954:
OHV & SV 250cc, 350cc, 500cc & 600cc, Groups B, C & M

BSA SINGLES (BOOK OF) 1955-1967:
B31, B32, B33, B34 and "Star" B40 & SS90

BSA 250cc SINGLES (BOOK OF) 1954-1970:
B31, B32, B33, B34 and "Star" B40 & SS90

BSA TWINS (BOOK OF) 1948-1962:
All 650cc & 500cc twins

BSA TWINS (SECOND BOOK OF) 1962-1969:
All 650cc & 500cc, A50 & A65 OHV unit construction twins

DUCATI OHC FACTORY WORKSHOP MANUAL:
160 Junior Monza, 250 Monza, 250 GT, 250 Mark 3, 250 Mach 1, 250 SCR & 350 Sebring

HONDA 250 & 305cc FACTORY WORKSHOP MANUAL:
C.72 C.77 CS.72, CS.77, CB.72, CB.77 [HAWK]

HONDA 125 & 150cc FACTORY WORKSHOP MANUAL:
C.92, CS.92, CB.92, C.95 & CA.95

HONDA 90 (BOOK OF) ALL MODELS UP TO 1966:
All 90cc variations including the S90, CM90, C200, S65, Trail 90 & C65 models

HONDA 50cc FACTORY WORKSHOP MANUAL: C.100

HONDA 50cc FACTORY WORKSHOP MANUAL: C.110

HONDA (BOOK OF) MAINTENANCE & REPAIR 1960-1966:
50cc C.100, C.102, C.110 & C.114 ~ 125cc C.92 & CB.92
250cc C.72 & CB.72 ~ 305cc CB.77

LAMBRETTA (BOOK OF) MAINTENANCE & REPAIR:
125 & 150cc, all models up to 1958, except model "48".

LAMBRETTA (SECOND BOOK OF) MAINTENANCE & REPAIR:
125, 150, 175 & 200cc, all Li & TV models and derivates from 1958 to 1970.

MATCHLESS SINGLES (BOOK OF) 1945-1956:
350 & 500cc OHV Touring Singles G3L, G80, G3LS & G80S

MATCHLESS SINGLES (BOOK OF) 1955-1966:
350 & 500cc OHV Touring Singles G3LS, G3S, G3, G80S, G80, Mercury, Mercury Sports, Major & Major Sports

NORTON DOMINATOR TWINS (BOOK OF) 1955-1965
500, 600 & 650cc Dominator Twins and 750cc Atlas

NORTON FACTORY TWIN CYLINDER WORKSHOP MANUAL:
1957-1970: *Lightweight Twins:* 250cc Jubilee, 350cc Navigator and 400cc Electra and the *Heavyweight Twins:* Model 77, 88, 88SS, 99, 99SS, Sports Special, Manxman, Mercury, Atlas, G15, P11, N15, Ranger (P11A).

NORTON (BOOK OF) MAINTENANCE & REPAIR 1932-1939:
All Pre-War SV, OHV and OHC models: 16H, 16I, 18, 19, 20, 50, 55, ES2, CJ, CSI, International 30 & 40

SUZUKI 200 & 250cc FACTORY WORKSHOP MANUAL:
250cc T20 [X-6 Hustler] ~ 200cc T200 [X-5 Invader & Sting Ray Scrambler]

SUZUKI 250cc FACTORY WORKSHOP MANUAL: 250cc ~ T10

TRIUMPH (BOOK OF) MAINTENANCE & REPAIR 1935-1939:
All Pre-War single & twin cylinder models: L2/1, 2/1, 2/5, 3/1, 3/2, 3/5, 5/1, 5/2, 5/3, 5/4, 5/5, 5/10, 6/1, Tiger 70, 80, 90 & 2H. Tiger 70C, 3S & 3H, Tiger 80C & 5H, Tiger 90C, 6S, 2HC & 3SC, 5T & 5S and T100

TRIUMPH 1937-1951 WORKSHOP MANUAL (A. St. J. Masters):
Covers rigid frame and sprung hub single cylinder SV & OHV and twin cylinder OHV pre-war, military, and post-war models

TRIUMPH 1945-1955 FACTORY WORKSHOP MANUAL NO.11:
Covers pre-unit, twin-cylinder rigid frame, sprung hub, swing-arm and 350cc, 500cc & 650cc.

VELOCETTE (BOOK OF) MAINTENANCE & REPAIR:
Covers LE Mk. I, II, & III, Valiant, Vogue, MOV, MAC, KSS, KTS, Viper, Venom & Thruxton. Includes some limited material on the Viceory scooter

VESPA (BOOK OF) MAINTENANCE & REPAIR 1946-1959:
All 125cc & 150cc models including 42/L2 & Gran Sport

VINCENT WORKSHOP MANUAL 1935-1955:
All Series A, B & C Models

COMING SOON IN THIS SAME SERIES:

BRIDGESTONE FACTORY WORKSHOP MANUAL: 50 Sport, 60 Sport,
90 De Luxe, 90 Trail, 90 Mountain, 90 Sport, 175 Dual Twin & Hurricane

BRITISH MILITARY MAINTENANCE & REPAIR MANUAL:
Service & Repair data for all British WD motorcycles

BRITISH MOTORCYCLE ENGINES: By the staff of "The Motor Cycle"

CEZETTA 175cc MODEL 501 SCOOTER MANUAL & PARTS BOOK

VILLIERS ENGINE WORKSHOP MANUAL: All Villiers engines through 1947

BSA BANTAM (BOOK OF) 1948-1970:
D7, D7D/L, D10, D14/4 & Bantam 175

HONDA 50 (BOOK OF):
C100, C102, C110, C114, P50, PC50, PF50, C50 (Also applicable to C100 Series Monkey Bike and CE105H Trail Bike

Please check our website at
www.VelocePress.com
For our most up-to-date listing

www.ingramcontent.com/pod-product-compliance
Lightning Source LLC
Chambersburg PA
CBHW070551170426
43201CB00012B/1800